A Yankee Private's
Civil War

Private Robert Hale Strong

A Yankee Private's
Civil War

Robert Hale Strong

Edited by Ashley Halsey

Dover Publications, Inc.
Mineola, New York

Bibliographical Note

This Dover edition, first published in 2013, is an unabridged republication of the work originally published by Henry Regnery Company, Chicago, in 1961.

Library of Congress Cataloging-in-Publication Data

Strong, Robert Hale, 1842–1928.
    A Yankee private's Civil War / Robert Hale Strong ; edited by Ashley Halsey. —Dover edition.
        p. cm.
    Originally published: 1961.
    ISBN-13: 978-0-486-49713-6
    ISBN-10: 0-486-49713-5
    1. Strong, Robert Hale, 1842–1928. 2. United States. Army. Illinois Infantry Regiment, 105th (1862–1865) 3. United States—History—Civil War, 1861–1865—Personal narratives. 4. Illinois—History—Civil War, 1861–1865—Personal narratives. 5. United States—History—Civil War, 1861–1865—Campaigns. I. Halsey, Ashley, editor. II. Title.

E505.5105th .S77 2013
973.7'8—dc23

                                                      2012041700

Manufactured in the United States by Courier Corporation
49713501   2013
www.doverpublications.com

Contents

Foreword   ix

Prologue   1

We March Off to Wipe Treason from the Earth   5

Action at Last: The Bullets Hum Like Bugs   12

Under Fire Every Day for an Age   19

Kennesaw Mountain Was an Awful Place   33

We "Bummers" Go Foraging   42

If You Can't "Pick" Rebs, "Pick" Yanks   57

What an Army Hospital Was Like   71

Discipline Makes War Hell   80

We March from Atlanta to the Sea   97

A Private Cease-Fire along the Chattahoochee   116

"Our Bullets Will Make Sieves of Your Hides . . ."   134

We Head Through South Carolina   157

War Continues to Be Hell   170

We Fight Our Last Big Battle   181

Our Last Long March Proves a Killer   201

Homeward Bound, but Still Fighting   213

Illustrations

Frontispiece

Map of the line of Sherman's march 22

Engravings

Sherman's Bummers foraging 48

The Capitol at Milledgeville, Georgia 69

Union Troops raise the flag atop the Governor's
House—Milledgeville, Georgia 69

Union Troops destroying a railroad 99

Building a corduroy road in the woods 103

Skirmishing in the woods 124

Confederates attack a wagon train 131

Scene at the crossing of a stream on an
improvised bridge 147

Foraging in Georgia 167

Union Pickets approached by Confederates
disguised in cedar bushes 188

Photographs following page 62

Major General William T. Ward

Major General Joseph Hooker

Fortifications and approaches to Kennesaw
Mountain, Tennessee

General Kilpatrick and his staff

Union troops guarding a railway bridge

Yankees doing camp chores

General Henry Warner Slocum

General Oliver Otis Howard

Rebel fortifications and approaches to Atlanta

The city of Atlanta

Photographs following page 158

General William T. Sherman

"Sherman's March To the Sea"—
·engraving by Ritchie

General Sherman and his staff

A Yankee pontoon bridge

City of Savannah, Georgia

General Joseph Eggleston Johnston

General John Bell Hood

The Capitol at Columbia, South Carolina

View from the Capitol

General William T. Sherman and his staff
at war's end

Foreword

THIS IS the story of a war fought by the youthful soldiers of a young nation. There was never another war like it in America, and we can hope and pray that there never will be again.

Most of the 2,500,000 Federal and 1,000,000 Confederate soldiers were not old enough to vote, but one in seven was old enough to die like a man. There were few "beat" youngsters among them even in the regiments which the Union raised from ex-slaves. Northerner and southerner alike usually needed no urging to go into battle. In combat, they fired with cold-eyed accuracy. Unlike some 20th century American infantry who could not or would not shoot at all, the boys in blue and gray shot to kill. They had no modern inhibitions; the word itself had not been invented. War meant kill or be killed. So they ran up the highest death rate in any of our conflicts.

One reason for the unstinted ferocity on both sides was that these millions were mostly youths proving themselves in a day when proof was required. They stood at the threshold of manhood and too many paid for admission with their lives. Cowardice was never more unstylish, nor casual bravery more current. Time and again, groups of enlisted men sought out the enemy and waged their own little battles without an officer present at all.

A distinctive thing about this book is that it is told entirely from the viewpoint of a private. Robert Hale Strong, who relates this tale, was a 19 year-old

farm boy in northern Illinois when his father decided
he could be spared from the crops to go to war with
the 105th Illinois Volunteer Infantry. Strong made
an exceptional private. He took to war with him not
only a shrewd American humor which smacks at times
of Mark Twain's but an instinctive skill in reporting
what he saw. And because he was always volunteering
to forage or picket, he saw far more than the average
soldier tramping along in dusty ranks.

As an associate editor handling *The Saturday Evening Post's* war centennial series, I read hundreds of
unpublished manuscripts. Of them all this gave the
best and clearest insight into how the war really
looked to a foot-slogging infantryman whom circumstances at times reduced to the level of a wild beast
but who never forgot home, mother, decency and
humanity.

Strong in his account reduces the role of citizen-
soldier to hardshouldered realism. He refers con-
sistently to combat of the bloodiest sort as "work." It
was "our work"—charging into the muzzles of an
enemy battery. It was "pretty hard work"—fighting
through mud and across enemy entrenchments. It was
"work we knew was cut out for us." And the work was
not eight or twelve hours, but twenty-four hours.

Strong returned home unwounded at the close of
the war, but never recovered from the rheumatism
contracted while sleeping in the rain. Bouts of it
racked him so badly that he moved from Illinois to
Arkansas in search of a warmer climate. During one
long siege of rheumatism, he began writing in re-
sponse to a promise to his mother to tell his war ex-

periences. She produced packets of his letters and wartime diaries which she had carefully saved. Refreshing his memory from these, he wrote his story in fits and snatches, at times stopping when he did not feel well enough to hold a pen. His mother transcribed his notes in longhand into composition books.

Strong's daughter, Mrs. J. M. Bill, of Ozark, Arkansas, preserved the original manuscript. Her daughter, Mrs. Jeanne Ross, of Warren, Arkansas, typed it up. In its original form, it ran 130 manuscript pages without a paragraph but the words flowed just as Strong had spoken them nearly a hundred years ago.

ASHLEY HALSEY, JR.

A Yankee Private's
Civil War

A Regular Soldier's Song

Hunger and thirst, hunger and thirst;
Give my my pipe, let 'em do their worst.

Cold and wet, cold and wet;
Give me my pipe, I soon can forget.

Sickness and pain, sickness and pain;
Give me my pipe, and I won't complain.

Powder and ball, powder and ball;
Give me my pipe, I'll smoke till I fall.

Battle and blood, battle and blood;
Give me my pipe, it'll still taste good.

Wounds and death, wounds and death;
I'll draw on my pipe with my dying breath.

Prologue

WELL, MOTHER, I did not think, when I told you last night that I would begin my recollections of the war when I was too lame to work, that the time would come so soon. But here I am, laid up for a while. So I shall start talking and you start writing. Will you want all I can remember? If I had a gift at story telling, I might maybe make it interesting.

Let's see, to begin . . .

I remember the excitement when news first came that the South had seceded. Indignation was felt by all except Copperheads and dough-faced Democrats. I remember the public meetings in the churches and farmhouses: how G.F. and his father blew the fife and beat the drum and exhorted the men to rally 'round the flag. I remember, too, how G.F. and his father did not do any "rallying" themselves, but stayed at home and raised wheat and corn and pork for a big price, for the government to buy for the boys who did rally.

I remember how Father told me, when I asked him to let me enlist, that he would let me go when he thought I was needed; and how I thought the war would be over before I would get a chance to win any glory. How large I felt when Father said to me one day, "If you still wish to enlist, now is the time for you to go."

I walked straightway to Naperville and wrote my name as big as any man—I was going on nineteen—on the page among the other heroes. I remember how

long a time it seemed to me before we were finally
ordered to rendezvous at Dixon, and how you and
Father took me to Wheaton where I, in company with
my future comrades, was to take the train to Dixon to
go into camp for instruction and drill. The first night
in Dixon, we found that no barracks had been prepared for us and we had as yet drawn no blankets. So
we had to go to hotels and pay our own bills. We were
ready, but the army was not ready for us.

The first meals issued us at Dixon were something
to remember, too. We were supplied only with a tin
cup and tin plate, nothing more. We fell into line and
marched up to the cook house and had our cups filled
with coffee and our tin plates filled with bean soup.
A loaf of bread was given each of us. We had no
spoons, no knives, no forks. What a time we had,
drinking soup from a tin plate. Try it sometime and
see how much you will spill. Before the next meal,
most of us had spoons, knives and forks.

Chat Smith and George Brown were the only ones
in the company from our own neighborhood. Mr. and
Mrs. Smith called on Chat while we were there. Then
when we had been ordered to Chicago and had gone
into camp there, you called on me, and Father came
up from Joliet, where he was on jury duty. He reached
camp at night, after Chat and I had retired. After
Father found me, we tried to wake Chat up to go to
town and sleep in a bed once more, but could not
wake him.

Many friends called on me at the camp, including
several girls, Gussie Cady for one. There were also a
number of girls and boys with whom I became ac-

quainted when at school at Lake Forest. We had visitors of a far different and less desirable kind, too. I remember how the gamblers used to come to camp, to prey on us innocent country boys, until we finally got mad and ran them off. And I remember ten thousand other things that would not interest you.

By this time, Uncle Sam had furnished us almost everything but guns. Uncle issued to us two big woolen blankets and a rubber blanket; two coats, one a dress coat with short, stiff collar and padded breast and shoulders, and the other a blouse; two shirts, two pair of drawers, two pair of socks. We had not as yet drawn any overcoats, as this was only the last of September.

Most of us had several changes of clothing, a large supply of knicknacks, a portable writing desk and writing material, and pictures of friends. Some brought revolvers to shoot the Rebels when they came to close quarters. Others, myself among them, had huge knives with which we would—in our minds—carve the whole Southern Confederacy. How big we did feel!

Much of any war is waiting. After frenzied preparations for combat, everything halts. Servicemen of World War II reduced it to a phrase: "Hurry up and wait." It applied equally in the Civil War. Bob Strong's company was mustered into the Union Army September 2, 1862. For eighteen months, it served on garrison duty in Kentucky and Tennessee and sampled the debatable joys of behind-the-lines life. Not until February, 1864, did it get to the front.

 ## we march off to wipe treason from the earth

WHEN WE left Chicago, we were sent to Louisville, Kentucky. On the way there, our train stopped in the early morning at Indianapolis. Some of us, Henry Rolf and I with others, left the train to get something to eat. Pretty soon, we saw a girl some twelve or fourteen years old looking at the train of soldiers. We asked her if she knew where we could get some milk. We asked the right person. Yes, she said, her father ran a dairy and never refused a soldier milk. So we went with her, just a short ways. Her mother met us at the door, took us in, gave us both a bowl of bread-and-milk, and refused to take any pay for it. Both of them at parting, said, "God bless you and all soldier boys."

On reaching Louisville, we stayed in camp only two days. Then we were ordered to march to Frankfort, Kentucky, to drive the Rebs away from that vicinity. From that time, we commenced to march in earnest. At Frankfort we drew our guns, cartridge and cap boxes, belt to carry them, and forty rounds of cartridges to every man. Added to our blankets, haversacks, canteen, clothing, which came to sixty-eight pounds, and extras including books, pictures, writing materials, etc., our load must have averaged over eighty pounds to a man, or rather, to a boy, for most of us were under twenty-one years of age. We were pretty well loaded, and no danger of playing much after our march each day was over.

I shall never forget how heavy my load got before we stopped for dinner the day we left Louisville. I thought the straps of my knapsack would pull my shoulders out of joint. The straps of my haversack (smaller bag) and canteen seemed no bigger than a thread, and were cutting the top of my shoulders. My gun seemed to weigh a ton. Never before nor since did I see *such a heavy gun!*

By the time we halted for dinner, everyone knew more about soldiering than they did in the morning. Nearly everyone went through their goods, emptying what they could best spare. I remember going through mine, but as tired and sore as I was, I could find nothing to spare. During the afternoon, though, I threw away one blanket. That night, no one had any difficulty in finding plenty of stuff that they could spare. It was said that a number of Jews followed the army with wagons and picked up big loads of clothing and other stuff. I know the people, living along the route, picked up lots of stuff.

That second night, Chat Smith got sick and I was left to take care of him and bring him on as soon as he was able to travel. His illness was only a touch of colic, so we resumed, he and I, some time in the A.M. We persuaded the planter at whose house we were left to send a nigger and a one-mule cart to help us on our way. We reached camp after night, and had a hard time to find our company.

At this point, we did some thinking. We had left home burning with a desire to wipe treason from the earth, and in fear that the war would be over before we could get into it. I remember Al Fisher of my company warning us boys not to be too anxious. He spoke of how boys watered elephants, carrying buckets and buckets, to get into the circus free. "Don't be impatient, boys, to see the elephant," Al said. "You will see him soon enough and you won't like him a damn bit, either." And he was right.

The very next night, I found myself on picket duty. I was posted at the extreme left flank, a scary spot. My beat extended along a fence almost to a swamp. The man whom I relieved said he had heard suspicious noises in the swamp, and advised me to keep my eyes wide open. After I had been there some time, I heard noises. Of course, orders were very strict not to fire unless at the enemy.

A good many pickets had been shot by the enemy while on post. Yet our orders were to "halt" everybody three times and, if not obeyed, to fire. The balance of the picket post and the reserve would then rush to the spot, but so many needless alarms had been given that we were told to be cautious.

Well, as I kept walking my beat I saw something moving in among the trees, but could not tell what it was. It did not take me long, alone in the middle of the black night, to make up my mind that it was someone hunting the picket to kill him. As I came back to the end of my beat next time, I plainly saw the enemy by moonlight. I watched him a few moments. He had worked himself quite close to my beat or path. There were several of them. They, as I approached, evidently thought they were discovered and moved off a little. I followed them carefully until quite a ways from my beat, when I ordered them to halt. Then I shot one of them so dead he never *squealed*.

The reserve came up on the run, and wanted to know what I had fired at. I told them something or someone moving in the brush. Another squad came up and the long roll or drumbeat summoning everyone to arms sounded in camp. Nothing was to be found, though, and all soon settled down. Then I quietly passed the word to our own boys in the company of what I had actually seen and shot, for I knew pretty well what I had done. They came up and cut the hams and shoulders from the dead "enemy," and for breakfast we had fresh ham steak. Even Put Scott, our company lieutenant, had a piece. That was the first blood I shed during the war, but not the last. Oh, dreadful!

The next day we entered Franklin, driving the Rebs out without a fight. We charged over a bridge

which they, on retiring, had set on fire. We put out
the fire and saved the bridge. Then we went back into
camp at Frankfort and drilled and drilled and drilled
some more.

Nothing much of importance happened while we
lay at Frankfort, except that we made a number of
trips after the Rebel General John Morgan. At one
time we were started in a terrible hurry at one A.M.
and marched eighteen miles, part of the way on the
run, and reached a point where we could see Morgan's
camp. The officer in charge of us ordered up a battery
and fired at the sleeping camp, thereby notifying
Morgan that the enemy was near. He just mounted
his men and fled. We, without any rest at all, turned
about and marched back to Frankfort without firing
a gun. We marched the thirty-six miles between one
A.M. and three o'clock the next afternoon—pretty
good for comparatively green troops.

At Frankfort there is, or was, the best kept and best
laid out cemetery I ever saw, with the finest monu-
ments, etc. I visited the tomb of Daniel Boone, and
from a cedar tree growing in the enclosure I whittled
out a matchbox and sent it to brother Albert. I don't
know what became of it. He never received it.

Our life was uneventful and consisted of camp
duty, that is, cleaning camp and sweeping the streets;
or picket duty, and the everlasting drill. Our camp
was always laid out in streets. Each company occupied
a street, so that each regiment had ten streets. Officers'
quarters at the head or front, cook house at the rear.

Up to the time we left Frankfort we had large tents,
which when we moved were carried on wagons. But

when we left Frankfort, each man was given the half of a shelter tent—pup tent, we called them—and we had to carry them ourselves. Each half was a little smaller than a sheet, but heavier stuff, with a row of buttons and buttonholes on three sides, and eyelet holes with looped rope on the fourth side. The buttons and buttonholes were to connect two or more half tents together, and the ropes were to hold the tents in position by means of pegs driven in the ground. Two of the halves buttoned together and stretched over a pole made a shelter from dew, but were not much shelter from rain. Six of them, the length of two with one at each end, would hold six men by a little crowding.

The night before we left for Bowling Green, Kentucky I was on guard duty, and I never saw a harder snowstorm. When the guards walked their beat they kept the snow packed. On each side of their path, the snow was two feet deep in no time. We finally went into camp at Gallatin, Tennessee. The mud was deep, the season unhealthy, and between guard duty and chasing Morgan, the men sickened and died rapidly. The dead march was played every day as someone from the regiment was buried.

In the fall of '63, our regiment was sent to do garrison duty near Nashville. Four companies were stationed in Fort Negley. The other six companies were stationed just outside the fort. Our duty there consisted in providing pickets and occasionally furnishing guards for railroad trains carrying ammunition and supplies to the front. The rail head was at first at Bridgeport, then at Stevens, Alabama.

Then the scene changed again. At Chattanooga—I

think it was in February, 1864—we were ordered to the front. We marched all the way over ground fought over by Generals Buell and Bragg. For miles and miles the road was full of dead horses and mules that had been killed or had given out along the way. One day after marching over the dead bodies of mules all day, we went into camp on the bank of a small stream just at dark.

It was my turn to procure water to cook our supper with, so I took our mess canteens and coffee pot down to the stream. I was fortunate to find an old log extending a little ways into the creek, so I stood on the log and filled my vessels. We made coffee, ate our supper and went to bed. The next morning I went back by daylight for water for our day's march, and found that the "log" that I stood on the night before was a dead and rotting mule. It was raining, and the rain had been running off the mule's body, and our coffee had been partly mule soup. I filled my canteens at another place this time.

Shortly thereafter, we went into camp permanently at the foot of Lookout Mountain near the spot where they fought the famous "Battle Above the Clouds." Our camping place was called Wauhatchie Valley. On the north of us loomed up mountains; on the south was Wauhatchie Creek, and just over the creek was Lookout Mountain. I spent many a day fishing from an old ruined mill dam in the creek. Chattanooga was about five miles from us, and just beyond *it* was Rebeldom.

I could tell many an anecdote of our camp life, but you want to hear of our March to the Sea, Mother, so I must hurry on or I will never get to it.

Early in 1864, Union strategy called for another vertical split in the Confederacy. The Mississippi River campaign had cut off southern states beyond the river. Now a massive Union force under William Tecumseh Sherman prepared to drive another wedge—down from Tennessee through Georgia to the sea. The move would sever another portion of the Confederacy. One of more than 100,000 bluecoats in it was Bob Strong, private, Company B, 105th Illinois Infantry.

 ## action at last: the bullets hum like bugs

IN THE spring of 1864, our regiment, the 105th Illinois, was consolidated with other troops and became part of the First Brigade, Third Division, 20th Army Corps. Major General Joe Hooker commanded the corps. Brigadier General William T. Ward commanded our brigade, which consisted of the 102nd, 105th and 129th Illinois, and the 79th Ohio and 70th Indiana. This last was commanded by Colonel Benjamin Harrison.*

Soon our first little brush with the enemy came. It was at Buzzards' Roost, a mountain pass in upper

* Editor's note: Later President Harrison.

Georgia. Up to this time we had had no big fights and had lost no men by bullets although we had been at "war" for nearly two years.

About this time, Company B, my company, was on scout. We halted for dinner on a bluff overlooking a creek, with a field beyond the creek and woods beyond that. Just after we halted, we heard a peculiar noise in the tree tops. It sounded like a lot of tumble bugs flying through the air. We wondered what caused the noise. Then small twigs began to drop near us. Then we heard guns going off and knew the "tumble-bug" noise was bullets. No one was hit. But it was soon to come.

On May 20th, the army advanced nearly to Resaca, Georgia. Our brigade was ordered to the right flank to support the troops engaged in fighting there. I distinctly remember how plain we could hear the whole business: the roar of the artillery, the crack of musketry, the cheers of the Yankees and the yells of the Johnnies. Through it all, we were lying in a thick wood and could see nothing. When we would hear the Yankees cheer, our hearts would almost stop beating. Then would come the roar of Rebel cannon, and as our boys were beaten back the Rebs would nearly split their throats yelling.

We lay there in a fever of impatience until our turn came. We marched around to the left,* and were

* Editor's note: Here we quote from RIFLE AND LIGHT INFANTRY TACTICS, Article 1 Paragraph 1, *Formation of a Regiment in order of battle, or in line:* "1. A regiment is composed of ten companies, which will habitually be posted from right to left, in the following order; first, sixth, fourth, ninth, third, eighth,

ordered to unsling knapsacks and put them in a pile. We left a guard over them and marched almost to the edge of the woods. My company, B, was ordered to advance as skirmishers—that is, in a thin, spread-out line well ahead of the main advance. Skirmishers are likely to see more of the world than anyone else, up to the point when they are suddenly shot.

We were told that just in our front was a Rebel fort that had been charged repeatedly, and every charge had been repulsed. Now *we had to take it.* Well, we knew there was "death in the pot" for some of us, wounds of all awful sorts for more of us, and supposed glory untold for the ones who came out alive. We were given forty extra cartridges to a man, and were told not to fire a gun until ordered to do so.

Company B, deployed as skirmishers, led the way out of the woods into an open field and then the work began. We were to advance in a steady line with guns at "shoulder arms" until the order to charge was given. Then the skirmishers were to lie down and let the column charge over us.

We first had to cross a small field and then go through a scattered peach orchard. Then, on a hill beyond, the fort sat waiting. As soon as we skirmishers moved out of the woods onto the field, the Rebs began

---

fifth, tenth, seventh, second, according to the rank of captains." This standard arrangement invariably placed Strong's Company B, or second company, on the extreme left. The arrangement is set forth in a manual for Ohio militia published at Cincinnati April 23, 1861, by T. Worthington, a former West Pointer, and dedicated to his West Point roommate, Major Robert Anderson, who only ten days earlier had surrendered Fort Sumter.

shooting at us. Someone cried out that there was a sharpshooter in a tree sniping at us. So, in spite of our orders not to fire, a dozen of us fired into the tree. The man came tumbling down, legs spread out, and struck the ground with a thud. I remember thinking as he fell that he resembled a big squirrel.

We advanced with no more shooting on our part. The bugle sung out "Skirmishers, lie down," and in the next minute, "Charge!" and the rest of the boys went over us with a yell. Most of the skirmishers, I among them, got up and joined the charging column and went up the hill with the rest. We were driven back from the works once, but in a moment we rallied and without waiting for orders—men were dropping all around us, but we had no time to look after them— with a rush and a cheer, which I can imagine I hear now, we drove the Rebs from the first line of works back into the second line, where their cannon were.

The hill was so steep that the cannon fired over the first line. Then we were reinforced by the Second Brigade, and we kept on going and drove the Rebs from their guns. Our brigade was ordered back, leaving the Second Brigade to hold what we had gained. You have a history of the rebellion which says the Second Brigade made this charge, but the writer of that history is mistaken. They held the line after we had captured it.

A great many amusing and pathetic incidents happened during and after our charge, only a few of which I will repeat. Undoubtedly you remember the massacre of the prisoners captured at Fort Pillow, Kentucky, by the Rebel General Nathan Bedford

Forrest. Well, when we rushed from the first line that we captured to the second line, where the Rebel cannon were, we of course captured a good many prisoners. Some of the enemy who refused to run or surrender were killed there. Some crawled under the gun carriages to escape the storm of bullets and bayonets.

One big red-headed man, a cannoneer, crawled out and begged for quarter. He had his shirt off, and on one arm was tattooed in big letters, "Fort Pillow." As soon as the boys saw the letters on his arm, they yelled, "No quarter for you!" and a dozen bayonets went into him and a dozen bullets were shot into him. I shall never forget his look of fear.

When we were ordered back to the rear and left the Second Brigade to hold the guns that we had captured, the Johnnies had fallen back only as far as another line of works or entrenchments. The cannon were left between the line we captured and the one they still occupied, only a few rods in the rear, and neither they nor our own men could use them.

We fell back not in a body or line of battle as we had advanced, but in squads numbering as many as a hundred, with orders to gather together at a certain place. Leon Palmer and I fell back together. There was a good many dead on the ground, and we had gone only a little way when we heard someone call in a weak voice. We went towards the voice and found a lieutenant of G Company. He had one leg broken, and as he fell the leg doubled up under him. It was bent clear back and the bone stuck out through the flesh. He wanted water, and to have his leg straightened out. Oh, how he groaned and prayed! He was grit clear through, though, and would not let us carry him off the field. The bullets were flying around us as thick, seemingly, as hail. After doing what we could for him, we left him. I don't know what became of him.

When we got back as far as we were supposed to go, we found a line of men posted across the road to stay stragglers from going on farther. General Ward came along with his arm in a sling, and said, "Old Pap got it this time, boys." He was pretty drunk, and seemed to be proud of his wound.

The ambulance corps kept bringing the wounded back. Shells were still flying over us, some going far to the rear, some bursting right around us. Two men brought a wounded man on a stretcher and set him down near me. I had just lit my pipe, and Mark Naper came to me to get a light for his pipe. I turned my pipe upside down to put it on top of his pipe and knock some fire into his, when a shell exploded just over us. A piece of it came down directly between us, breaking both pipes. Another piece killed the wounded man who was on the stretcher. It surely was a close call for Mark and me.

It was during this battle that Lieutenant Colonel Henry F. Vallette, next only to old Colonel Dan Dustin in our regiment, got so badly scared that he soiled his breeches. He never got over that scare. Anyway, he left us during our next fight and we never saw him again until we got home.

That night, they called for volunteers to bring off the guns that we had been unable to take during the day. A number volunteered and crept up to the breastworks. They dug with spades a gap in the breastworks wide enough to get the guns out and, attaching ropes to them, dragged them away. A lieutenant of some Ohio regiment had charge of the volunteers.

Later that same night, the Rebs left their works and started for another stronghold. Our brigade was detailed to bury the dead. Of all disagreeable jobs, that was the worst of any I ever took a hand in. It was our first experience, and to carry men to a hole and dump them in was almost too much for me. Some had been dead for three or four days, and the flesh would not hold together to lift them. So we put them in blankets, or tied the legs of their pants and their coatsleeves together and gently dragged them to their last resting place.

We came across a Rebel hospital with a few Rebel surgeons who had been left to care for their wounded. The hospital was simply a shade made of limbs of trees thrown over poles. Near the hospital was a pile of arms, legs, hands, and feet that had been cut from the wounded. These had not been buried, just thrown in a pile, and worms had begun to work on them.

On one part of the battlefield the leaves had taken fire, I suppose from shells, and we found a few of the dead who had more or less burned. It is all truly horrible, and if you tell me you don't want anything more on battle scenes, why all right. But so many things come to mind, some worse than these.

"My general plan now was to concentrate all the force possible against the Confederate armies in the field. . . . [One] under General Joseph E. Johnston, was at Dalton, Georgia, opposed to Sherman, who was still at Chattanooga. . . . Sherman was to move from Chattanooga, Johnston's army and Atlanta being his objective points."—General U. S. Grant.

 ## under fire every day for an age

WE WERE under fire every day for about a month, from Buzzards' Roost to Atlanta. While I remember every fight, I can't name all or nearly all the battlefields, it has been so long since I have thought of them. I don't mean that we were in a big fight every day, but were in at least a skirmish on the picket line. We were always firing at one another. All the way to Atlanta was a series of fights. We did not always have it our own way, the Rebels were as stubborn as mules. They had lines of entrenchments all the way.

The Rebs had niggers to build breastworks for them, and we had to build our own or go without. The sound of the axe was constantly heard, cutting timbers to line the works.

One day on the march, we came to a splendid line of works but found it empty. Just before we reached the works we saw a large tree with a hole made through it by a solid shot. Low down on the other side, sitting against the tree, was a headless man. He had been sitting there during the fighting, and undoubtedly thought himself safe, when a Yankee solid shot went through the tree and took his head off. His body remained against the tree. There was no trace of his head.

In one fight, I can't remember which one, a number of us were out in front of the regiment, forming a skirmish line to fend off the Rebs, while the regiment was building breastworks. We stayed out there until after dinner time, when we were relieved by some of the boys who crawled out to us on their hands and knees so as not to draw Rebel fire. We went in back of the breastworks and were eating our crackers and coffee when some of the men from the skirmish line came up with a rush. Some Rebels were attacking. Captain Scott says, "Boys, you will have to move." We jumped up. As we struck our feet, down went Elias Cook, shot through the breast. He lived just long enough to send word to his people. Things calmed down on the skirmish line, so we sat down again. Almost immediately, we had to rise and get ready to fight if needed. Elias Burns sang out, "The Rebel bullet is not yet made, that is to kill me." At that, he jumped up and fell down the same instant with a bullet in his brain. He fell across my lap—I was still sitting—and his brains and blood ran into my haversack, spoiling my rations. So I took his.

Scott says, "Run, some of you, for a stretcher." I started to the rear for one. To get to where the hospital tents were, I had to cross a little hill. The bullets and shells were plowing up the ground on that hill so thick and fast that you could hear the stones they hit rattling. As I started up the hill, the colonel saw me going and halted me and wanted to know where I was headed. I told him. He says, "Go on if you must, but I won't have a boy left by night; you will never get over that hill alive!" But I did, and got back again.

At the same place the next day, I was again on the skirmish line. A fellow from another company, by the name of Grant, got together with me and we watched a certain rifle pit of the Rebs and agreed to devote our attention to that pit. By noon, we had silenced the rifles from that pit. Just to the left of me, there was a big tree behind which the skirmishers would get, but some Rebel sharpshooter had a range on it and he killed a great many men there. One man was hit, and when the stretcher bearers come and got him and started to the rear, both bearers were shot and killed, the hind one falling forward onto the wounded man.

Of course, you will understand that much more happened during this time that I have been telling about. I can tell of only a few things that I took part in. There were many serious things and many funny things that happened. There was a great deal of card playing and gambling in other ways, and a great deal of praying. Our chaplain preached to us and prayed for and with all the boys that would let him.

Our marches on the campaign between Chattanooga

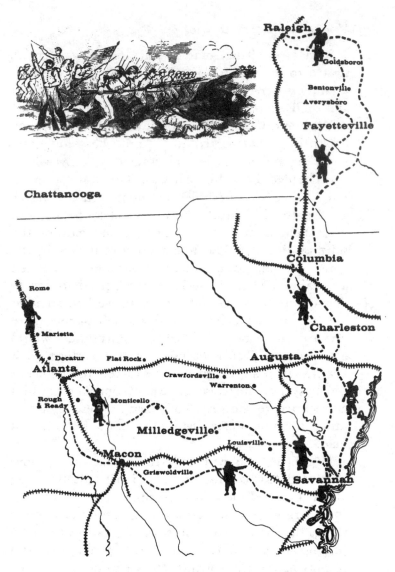

Broken lines show the march of Sherman's armies as they swept down from Tennessee through Georgia. The route widened at Atlanta and turned left at Savannah into the Carolinas.

Railroads ┼┼┼┼┼┼┼┼┼┼┼┼┼┼┼┼┼┼┼┼┼┼┼

and Atlanta were not long but were often hard. We slept in full harness, without removing shoes or belts, ready at any time for action. It rained a great deal, and for days and days we would not have a dry thread on us. Many and many a time have I piled rocks together to keep me out of the water while I slept. We could not draw new clothing when we wanted it now, and many of us were as good as barefoot.

In the morning, after sleeping on the wet ground and it raining all night, we would, if we had the time, build a big fire and try to dry our tents and blankets before we rolled them up. If we did not have time, we rolled them up wet and then they would be heavy as lead to carry. Unless the sun came out and dried them during the day, that night we would have to lie down wet through and put our wet blankets over us.

Many nights we had no time to put up our little tents, and if we did they were but little protection in a storm. Still, through it all, it is surprising how good-natured nearly everyone was. I remember one morning, after sleeping on the wet ground following a wet day's work, that the sun was shining when I woke up. I was lying on my back, and could not get up nor move hand nor foot, I was so lame and stiff from rheumatism. The boys helped me up, rubbed and slapped me a little until my blood got to circulating, and I was able to march on.

When it rained, the innumerable wagons with six mules to each wagon, the heavy artillery, the ambulances and the cavalry left the road in a horrid condition for foot soldiers. For days we would march with our pants stuck in our stockings and the stockings held up by strings, with the mud coming over the top of our shoes at every step. At such times, it was actually a relief to come to a small river with the bridge gone. We had no time to wash our clothes for weeks, and our camp washerwoman had not come with us.

As a consequence of having no washing done, that particular "friend of man" who stuck closer than a brother, caused us much annoyance. They would get into the seams of our shirts and pants and drawers, and when not engaged in laying eggs, would sally out and forage off our defenseless bodies. Next, he, his children and his children's children, with their brothers and sisters, would hold squad drill on our backs. At every leisure moment, the boys would pull off their shirts and such a cracking of thumbnails never took place anywhere but in the army. At every opportunity, we would strip ourselves and boil our clothes, and for a few days we would have peace. As none of us had but one suit of clothes by now, the spectacle we made at such times was somewhat ludicrous. While our clothes were boiling, some of the boys would put on a woolen blanket, some a rubber blanket, some nothing. Next to fighting and eating and sleeping, and perhaps praying and gambling, came washing. After being in a hard battle all day, we were always dirty. What with sweat and dust or burnt gunpowder, our own mothers would not have known us.

During this time, we became so used to noise, the firing of guns and cannon, the yelling and cursing of teamsters and artillerymen and the blaring of the bugles, that we would, when tired and permitted to do so, lay down and sleep amid it all. Only our brigade bugle call would rouse us. It was queer, but while sleeping in all this noise, let our bugle play out the first bar of "Hail Columbia," then every man would hear it. The brigade call was the first bar of the song, no more, but it was enough. After playing it, the brigade bugler would follow it up by whatever call he was ordered to make, and he was followed by the regimental buglers who took it up. In the morning it was reveille, or call to get up. After the buglers were all through, the regimental bands would take it up. Our regiment had also a drum corps, consisting of a bass drum, two or more snare drums, and several fifes. Our musicians were a kind-hearted, jolly set of boys, who during a battle wore a yellow ribbon on their arms to show they were noncombatants engaged only in carrying the wounded off the field. At reveille the musicians would march up and down in front of the regiment playing as if their lives depended on it. Then out the boys would tumble, or rather, jump.

We had three minutes to dress, if that was necessary, and to get in line for rollcall and doctor's call. Then to strike tents and march to breakast. Then "attention" and doctor's call for those who reported sick at rollcall. After that, we fell into line with accoutrements on, ready for the day's work.

During the first part of the Atlanta campaign, I messed with Mathias Stephens and Ernst Hymen, both good, quiet religious boys. One night after advancing and driving the enemy all day, my mess had eaten and gone to our pup tents. We were talking about the probability of a battle on the morrow. I used some strong language about the enemy and about our having to work so hard on short rations. Stephens checked me, saying: "Don't talk so. Some of us will be killed tomorrow in the fight."

Well, early the next morning we began a running fight, with the enemy falling back slowly. In advancing, we took advantage of all the shelter we could get, behind logs or stumps. My position was on the right of the company, being one of the tallest boys, but of course in that kind of advance ranks are not kept very true. It got to be a pretty hot fight. I heard someone call out, "Strong—Bob Strong!" Before I could answer, someone else says, "There he is, out there in front of the line." I saw the hit man shudder and lay his head down on his arm. I knew he undoubtedly was killed, for if only wounded he would have called further for help.

The Rebels refused to be driven any further for hours. It was nearly sundown when they pulled out and we advanced up. Our boys all gathered around the fallen man in our immediate front. Sure enough, it was one of my messmates, Ernst Hymen. He was shot directly through the top of his head and probably never knew what hurt him. He was a good boy and all liked him. Our orders were to push on after the enemy, but a few of us remained, dug a pit, and wrapped Ernst in a blanket in his lonely grave.

About this time, I was taken with rheumatism and camp diarrhea. I was often obliged to fall out of ranks for a little while. One day just as we were going into a fight, Lieutenant Willard Scott, Jr., Put Scott we always called him, who had command of the company, says to me, "R.H., you don't look fit to be with us, take this pass and fall out and stay out until night." I set down behind a tree. Pretty soon the boys struck the Rebs and heavy firing began. The shells and bullets whistled past me and sometimes struck the tree I was behind. I sat right there until I was rested. Then I rose to return to the rear, but stopped and said to myself: "The boys have not had a single fight without my being with them. If I go to the rear and am killed there, I will be ashamed to meet them on the other shore. I am going up to the company." When Put Scott saw me, he blowed up, but I stayed with them.

One day during a battle, our brigade was ordered from the center, where we had been held back in reserve, around to the right of the enemy. We marched just behind entrenchments filled with Yankees and across a field where we could see the enemy's breastworks. We watched them working their artillery, with their shell and shot whistling over and among us. At the rear of the regiment were the major, E. F. Dutton, and Dr. Potter, the brigade surgeon. If a shell came low, the men in line with it would lie down. One came along striking the ground and rebounding. Dr. Potter with others was directly in line. Some lay down. Dr. Potter laughed at the boys. The shell struck the ground just in front of him, rebounded, and took the top of his head off. As it hit him, a little puff went up from his head and he fell dead. Then the shell struck the ground a few feet beyond him and stopped, with the fuse hissing. One of our boys ran to it and poured water from his canteen onto the fuse, putting it out and thereby probably saving many lives at the risk of his own.

At that point, we were ordered off to the left to support a battery of ours. As we came in sight of the battery, the Rebs in three lines were charging it. They were about as near it as we were. We went on the run to save it. How those gunners did work those guns! At every discharge we could see great holes open in the Johnnies' ranks, but they closed up and kept on coming. When we reached our place behind the guns, the Rebs were not more than a hundred feet away. Even in our hurry and great danger, we handled our rifles as if on drill. Every man reached his place, pointed toward the enemy, and began firing. The Rebs were not more than sixty feet away. They went down in droves, like a boy shooting into a flock of blackbirds. It checked the charge, and the Rebs fell back. Our boys sent up a big cheer and a tiger, then the battery boys had to shake hands with such of us as they could reach.

The enemy infantry having pulled back, their artillery began firing at us. Our battery returned the fire. We of the infantry lay down so as not to catch any more of the shot and shell than we could help.

It was said that there were seven hundred dead and wounded on our front. I know the fields looked as if we could walk over men without putting foot to the ground. The fighting whenever we had to support a battery was always of the hardest, for guns were one thing the enemy really went after.

Once while we lay supporting a battery of ours on a

hillside, the enemy lay on the opposite hill, waiting to charge. In between us was an open field with a creek through it. While we lay there, the enemy formed in line to charge. Our battery opened on them with canister, and they scattered.

Then we were ordered to do a thing that I thought then, and think now, was a foolish, fool-hardy thing. Our music struck up, and with arms at "shoulder" we infantry marched in a solid square out into that open field with our bands playing "Behold, the Conquering Hero Comes." We. stood at rest in the field for half an hour, supposing every minute of the time that the Rebs would open fire on us as we were in plain view of their position. As they did not accept our challenge, we then marched up to where they had been an hour or less before, and found they had left.

Years afterward in Nebraska, where I moved after the war, another Union veteran, on finding that I belonged to these troops, said that our performance that day was the grandest thing he ever saw. He said his regiment lay to the left of us, but in full view of all, and that they just held their breath, expecting the Rebs would open on us and annihilate us.

Having occupied the Rebel position without resistance, we lay down expecting that we were safe for the rest of the day. Put Scott was marching up and down in front of us, declaiming some funny piece to amuse us, when suddenly the Rebs began to shell us. Scott kept on declaiming and the boys kept on laughing. Then with a big shock a heavy shell struck the ground in front of our company, within ten feet of us. It buried itself in the ground, and we just held our breath expecting it to explode. Scott threw himself on

the ground. I flattened myself out on the ground until
I seemed to have made a hole in it. Maybe you can
imagine what the suspense was, waiting for some of us
to be killed. Of course, all this happened quicker than
you can read it.

After perhaps a minute, Mark Naper lifted his head
and, with his eyes big as saucers, said, "Why don't the
d—d thing bust?" That made us laugh, and we began
to get up. As far as I know, that shell never has exploded yet.

On another day, as we were marching in column,
not spread wide in line of battle, we could hear the
musketry very plain and knew that our turn would
soon come. We marched into sight of the enemy's
works and they shelled us. Their range was good and
their shells and bullets kept us dodging busily. Now
you must understand that it was no use to dodge, as the
shells and balls would either hit or pass us quicker
than we could dodge.

Old Colonel Dustin, our regimental commander of
the 105th, saw the boys dodging and he sung out: "Stop
that dodging. Stop it, I say!" Just then along came a
shell pretty close to his head. He was on horseback and
he bowed his head almost to the saddle bow. The boys
laughed, whooped and yelled. The colonel straightened up and said, "Well, d—n it, dodge a little, then."

One fellow, Bill Purnell, went down with a groan
and clasped his foot in his hands. Scott says, "Got it,
Bill?" Bill says painfully, "Yes, tore my foot off." We
had no time to stop, so we left him with his shoe and
apparently part of his foot hanging in shreds. Half an
hour later, just as we had got warmed up to our work,
along came Bill, hardly limping. He was mad clear

through. The shell or shot had struck the toe of his shoe, literally cutting it to pieces, but had not drawn blood from his foot. It was surely a miraculous escape.

We fought them all that day. They were on an elevation, and it seemed to me that we experienced the heaviest firing that we had seen all through the war. After we had been relieved and had gone some distance to the rear, we could see round shot roll along the ground with enough force to shred a man's flesh, as one poor negro discovered who tried to stop one with his foot.

Again the next day, while lying down in the woods, the Rebs began to shell us. I saw one shell go through a tree forty feet above the ground. All I could see was a puff as it struck the tree, and I could see the bark fly as it came out. Soon they got a better range on us, and they just everlastingly put it to us.

One boy, laying on his face, says "Thunder!" He began to pull off his coat. We helped him. There on his shoulder blade was a lump as big as a goose egg and as soft as air. A piece of shell had hit, but flat, it seemed, for it did not go through his clothes. It left him lame for a week.

We moved, and lay behind a fence rail for an hour without doing any real work. Then we moved again, to the right. After the last move, I found I had lost my knife and my pocket book. I started back to the fence where we had last been, to look for them. When I got nearly there, I found the Rebs had taken possession of that place and I lost all desire to recover my property.

The second day of the fight, we had been advanced towards the enemy in the shape of an upside-down V, with our troops at the point and Rebs on each side and in front. We were in timber. Across an open field, we could see the Rebs massing for a charge about eighty rods away. The 102nd Illinois, armed with Spencer rifles, the famous seven-shooters, were deployed in front of us as skirmishers. They were in a thin, spread-out line as skirmishers usually are. As the Rebs would advance, the 102nd boys would open on them with their seven-shooters and pretty soon, back they would go, only to rally and try again. We could hear their officers cursing them for cowards to run from nothing more than a thin line of skirmishers.*

Our boys kept inviting the Rebs to come on. We could see them approach, see them fall, and pretty soon, back they would go. Shortly after they quit coming at us, General Joe Hooker rode up, looked around at our exposed position, and asked, "Who has command of these troops?" Brigadier General William T. Ward, who commanded our brigade, came up and said, "I have, sir." Hooker says, "D—n you, sir, don't you know you have got these boys in a trap? The enemy is on three sides of them, and prepared to charge on each side. Recall everybody but skirmishers and tell them to fall back quietly. Don't let so much as a tin cup rattle to tell the Rebs that we are moving." So we got out of that, but it was a close call.

---

* Editor's note: Here is a rare firsthand account of the effect of modern repeaters, firing rim-fire cartridges, on troops accustomed to facing nothing more rapid-fire than muzzleloaders. The Spencers had a rate of fire seven times that of the muzzleloaders. Hence a few skirmishers armed with them were as effective as a much larger force with regular muskets—a fact that the cursing Confederate officers either did not grasp or refused to recognize.

Figures in the furious campaign for Atlanta tell a story of awful bloodshed. Approximately one man in every four engaged on both sides was killed or wounded. Federal losses: 4,423 killed, 22,822 wounded. Confederate: 3,044 killed, 18,952 wounded. One of the bitterest engagements centered around a wooded rise, Kennesaw Mountain. A Confederate who survived named his squalling baby son Kennesaw Mountain Landis. The boy became a judge and big-league baseball's first "czar."

 ## kennesaw mountain was an awful place

WE WERE seven days getting old Johnston on the run at Kennesaw Mountain. He had entrenched himself behind strong fortifications on both Big and Little Kennesaw.

It was a grand and splendid sight at night to see the Rebel campfires and the artillery duels back and forth; to see our shells bursting amidst their campfires and to see their cannon, away up on the mountainside, burst forth in red flame. One moment the glare would show us trees, men, guns. The next minute all would be dark. We could watch the course of the shells by the lighted fuses, like huge fireflies. The shells revolved in their courses, then burst in the air, sending their contents hissing on ahead. It made a grand pyrotechnical display.

For us in the infantry, it was charge and countercharge both day and night. One night we were laying behind our breastworks, all asleep except the guards, who were pacing back and forth on top of the works. About ten o'clock, the officers came and woke every man by touching him. They whispered for us to take our places. A Rebel courier had been captured. His dispatches revealed that our lines were to be attacked between ten and twelve o'clock that night. So we had to move rapidly.

The guards were sent to the front with orders to listen for any sound. At any advance by the enemy, they were to come quickly behind the works and notify us without letting the enemy know their approach had been discovered. We were to hold our fire, both artillery and infantry, until the enemy came close to us, then pour it into them.

The dispatches we captured said a big gun was to be fired by the Rebs, way off, as a signal for them to attack us. Our officer said that if we heard the big gun, we could be sure they were coming. We were to be very alert and careful, whether the big gun went off or not. Sure enough, the big gun did go off. Everybody punched his neighbor, at that, to be sure no one had fallen asleep. Pretty soon the guards came crawling over the works and reported the Rebels were right behind them. In a minute, we could hear them.

Now our orders were that only number 1's, or the

odd numbers, were to fire at first. The number 2's, even numbers, were to hold their fire a minute. This would give us a loaded gun for every other man, and give us two close volleys instead of one. If the Rebs tried to quick-charge us after the first volley, thinking our guns were all empty, they would be in for a grim surprise.

The command came, "Take aim, aim low." Then, "FIRE!" and a solid sheet of flame burst out of the night. In a minute more, a second sheet of flame tore through the dark. The discipline was gone, and every man fired as fast as he could load. The Rebs rushed at us with yell after yell. The Yanks cheered and invited them to come on.

It was all over in less time than it takes to tell it. The Rebs went trotting back to cover—but a thousand of them never went back.

When we made a charge, it resulted in just about the same way. Each army was well entrenched and comparatively safe and snug.

One night we were lying back in the second line of entrenchments to rest. Our orders were to sleep with our arms by our sides, and not to remove any article of clothing, as another attack was expected. Cannon had been massed behind our front works. Ambulances were waiting, too. About midnight, the Rebs came charging up on the run to the front works. For a while, one could see to read by the artillery flashes. Although we knew the enemy was trying to break our lines and run over us, we had so much confidence in the boys in front, and in the strength of our works, that we never even rose to our feet. As soon as the fighting stopped, we went right back to sleep. I remember that my feet, at the time, were covered with blisters. To rest them, I had removed my shoes. At the first fire, I sat up, tightened my belts, and held one shoe in my hand ready to draw it on if the Rebs broke through our first line. They did not, and in twenty minutes we were all asleep again. I've known a fretting baby to keep its parents awake longer.

Artillery was a headache to us one way or the other a lot of the time. We had to help get ours out of the mud, then defend our batteries against Rebel charges. In the meantime their artillery would give us fits.

During some battle, I forget which, our brigade was lying in the rear and taking no part. The boys were sitting behind trees to avoid shells and bullets. Some were quiet, some were telling stories and cracking jokes, but all were listening to the shriek of the shells as they flew over us.

On a hill in our front was a Rebel battery that had been playing on us all day. We had for hours expected that we might be ordered to capture that battery. Sure enough, pretty soon along came an orderly enquiring for the commanding officer. We were ordered to unsling knapsacks and put them in a pile. Then we were ordered to fix bayonets and prepare to charge the battery.

"Sherman wants those guns," the order came to us. Mark Naper up and says, "Tell Sherman he can have them—we don't want them and will give him our title to them." Al Wiant looked up at the battery, then up and down our lines, and says: "Well, boys, if Old Billy wants them, he has got to have them. I say let's all chip in and go get the things for him." And so we did.

One time we were lying behind a battery of our own and supporting it. We were expected to repulse any charge the Rebs might make on the battery. While it was easy sitting it was dangerous work, because the enemy's batteries were shelling ours and our battery was shelling them.

Our artillerymen were stripped to the waist for their work. It was a sight to watch them firing those cannons. Each man at the cannon is numbered, and each number has just certain things to do. He does this with the regularity of clock work, and does nothing else. The caisson holding the ammunition is brought up to a few feet in rear of the cannon, the horses are unhitched and taken a short distance to the rear and hidden if possible, and firing begins.

One man brings the powder cartridge from the caisson. Another man shoves it into the cannon muzzle. Another one rams it down. By this time, the first man has returned from the caisson with a shot or a shell. If it is a shell and the fuse is already cut to the required length, the shell is passed on to the cannon, inserted and rammed home. If not properly fused, the fuse is adjusted first.

Then the priming is inserted in the touch hole and the string that fires the cannon is pulled. After the shell screams out and the cannon recoils, the cannon is run back into position. Then one man puts his finger over the touch hole to keep out air. Another with a swab or sponge on a pole wipes out the cannon. Another shell is inserted and fired. As this is done two or three times in a minute, everybody is on the jump.

Every so often, the end of the swab is dipped in a bucket of water and the cannon thoroughly washed out.* If an artilleryman is killed or wounded, another stands ready to take his place. Each is trained to do the next man's job when needed.

At this time we had a good view of the enemy's guns and of their lines behind. We could see our shells burst inside their lines. One shell knocked a wheel off one of their cannon. All this time, their shells were striking and bursting among us. Some of our gunner men were just literally blown to pieces. As they were, the next one would take his place. It was a grand sight, but a horrible one.

About this time, we were almost all of us whiskery. Abe Fisher borrowed my razor to shave some of the boys. He laid a board across two boxes. We were just behind the battle lines, lying in the rear but not so far in the rear. The bullets were flying thick around us. The one to be shaved straddled Abe's board, and he told us waiting ones to "get behind a tree and I'll call you when I want you."

As we turned away to the trees, a bullet struck Jimmie McMillan and down he went. After he had rolled over a couple of times, he yelled, "Jasus, I'm kilt. I'm dead." We turned him over. He was in his shirt sleeves and the blood was running out of a hole in his arm. Al Wiant says, "You ain't killed, Jim. It only went through the fleshy part of your arm."

---

* Editor's note: This is to prevent an accumulation of black-powder fouling, which impedes loading and accuracy and increases the risk of a premature discharge.

Up jumps Jimmie shouting, "The Virgin be praised. Now I'll get a furlough!" But in lifting his arm, we saw a hole in his shirt and *it* was bloody. When we called his attention to it, he fell down again and said, "Oh, Holy Mother, have pity, I'm kilt indeed. Oh, Saint Peter, save me!" We pulled his shirt off, and there was the bullet, stuck between two ribs. It must have been almost spent when it hit him. Someone pulled it out with his fingers.

Jimmie turned mad as fire. He got no furlough and did not even go to the hospital. Instead, he was given the company mule to lead, with its big pots and pans for cooking, while the man who had been leading the mule took Jim's place in the ranks.

Before that, Jimmie had been a good soldier. Afterwards, he was afraid of his own shadow. This mule carried two frying pans and the heavier cooking utensils of the boys, so it had to be brought up with us at night and at noon also if possible. Once, almost at night, while we were still fighting, Jimmie was ordered to bring the mule up to us. "I'll be d—d if I will," says Jim. "You will be d—d if you don't," says the man sent back for the mule. So Jim brought him up part way, got behind a tree, and told the boys to unload the mule.

The sergeant stepped up at that, and told Jim to unload the mule himself, and pushed him away from behind the tree. As Jim began to unload, a shell came along and struck the mule, grazing his back. A skillet whipped off and hit Jim, and he laid down swearing that he wouldn't unload the damn mule if he died for it.

He afterwards came back to regular duty in the company. One night we had both been on picket. We were relieved about daylight when our tent mates went on picket, so when we came in Jim and I crawled under the same pup tent. Jim says, "You take that side," motioning to the side towards the enemy.

I had just got to sleep when I heard a noise that sounded like the explosion of a gun. Jim began to yell, "I'm shot! I'm shot! Bad cess to them, how could they shoot over you and hit me?" A spent ball, dropping sharply downward at the end of its flight, had fallen through the tent. It struck him on the chest, raising a large bump but not breaking the skin.

We soldiers were not the only ones to get hit. Once I was on the skirmish line, driving the enemy. As they fell back, we advanced until we came to a house between the two lines. Of course, we supposed the house was unoccupied, as people usually cleared out in a hurry when shooting began. When we came to within fifteen or twenty rods of the house, a woman ran out right in the middle of the shooting.

The house sat on a hill, with the ground sloping away from it in both directions. Both the Rebs and us were shooting low. The woman had gone only a few rods from the house when down she went. She had been shot through the ankle. I think she was going for water for a wounded man who was in the house. Of course, neither side intended to shoot her. She merely ran against one of the many balls that were passing, and so she got hurt.

One day we were drawn up in line preparatory to advancing on the enemy. A call came for volunteers to go ahead at once and dislodge the enemy from some place. A number of us stepped to the front. Almost at that instant, the Rebs began shelling us. A piece of shell cut the haversack strap of Bill Purnell, the same man who had lost his shoe earlier. "They have cut my supply train," says Bill. Just then something twisted by my side. I looked. A bullet had torn through my canteen. "They have cut off my water supply," says I.

Among the boys who volunteered on this occasion were Leon Palmer and I. In some way, we became separated from our comrades. In looking for them, we fell in with a New York regiment. Just then, the Rebs made a rush for us. Leon and I asked the New York captain if he had room for us. "Yes," he says, so we took position with his boys. There was no place for us to lie down amongst the New York boys, so we had to take it standing. After the brush was over, I found that the button on one side of my cap had been shot off. The cloth star, our brigade insignia, that was pinned to my cap, had been cut by a bullet. Leon also had something of the kind to show, but neither of us was hurt.

After it was all over, the New York captain shook hands with us and said: "When I saw you coming I was about to order you arrested. I thought you were sneaks. Now I wish all my boys were such sneaks." Then we felt good and hunted our own boys.

On the upper part of its battle southward, from Chattanooga to Atlanta, Sherman's army received supplies regularly by railroad. Foraging or "bumming" was a sideline activity to procure fresh foodstuffs to supplement Army diet. It was also an avenue of escape from the duller duties of camp life and military routine.

 # we "bummers" go foraging

ALL OF our experiences in the war were not hard. We had lots of fun at times. Sometimes a detail would be sent to hunt something to eat, when our rations got low, which they did often. When out on such occasions, we really had fun.

One time when we had been out foraging in Georgia and pretty well cleaned one place of everything to eat, the lady of the house—there were no men there—accused us of stealing some jewelry. The captain in charge denied it. He said that if anything was stolen, she or her daughters or her niggers had got it, and he would be d—d if he didn't have them searched.

The old lady and several daughters and a dozen

nigger wenches were standing in the yard close to the house. The captain stormed around and ordered the wenches to get into line. They formed a crooked, straggly line. To form a better line, the captain sung out, "Close up, close up!" The wenches thought the personal search was about to begin, and that the order meant "Clothes up." So they began to giggle and simper, and lift their dresses—all the clothes they had on—pretty high.

"What are you doing, that ain't what I mean!" the captain quick sung out. Just then, one of the young ladies was so shocked, thinking she might be searched next, I suppose, that she spoke up and said she had hid jewelry to keep it away from the Yanks.

From that day on, we boys had only to call out to that captain, "Close up," to make him swear.

We one time found a woman, nice-looking, too, who had some apples. We bought so many of her that the barrel she got them out of began getting empty. It stood on a box in one corner of the house. In order to reach the apples in the bottom of the barrel, she got a three-legged stool, or as she called it, a piggin. The second she jumped up on it, it tipped. Over she went, head-first into the barrel. Well, it was impudent of us to do so, but we laughed and laughed. All I remember further was that her stockings were tied up with red rags.

Another time we went out after horses. Just as we came to a house, two or three men rode off into the woods. We fired at them, but they only went the faster. We then searched the house, but found no men. In the stable, we found two horses. One was old and worn-out, but one was a fine young horse and we confiscated it.

One of the young ladies thereupon begged us not to take the fine horse. She said it was a present from her dead father, and the only one left on the place fit for the women to ride to the mill. If we would leave it, she said, she and her sisters would treat us to a good dinner. So we agreed to leave the horse. We went and set on the porch while dinner was preparing.

While we were still setting and waiting, that same horse dashed out of the lot with a Rebel officer on him and sped into the woods and away from us safely. Oh, how the women did laugh at us for being fooled by a girl! The Reb officer had been hiding under the bed, which had curtains to it. When we put the horse back into the stable and went politely around and set on the front porch, he crawled out, left by the back door, and lost no time riding off.

The girls still said we should stay and have our dinner and take our time, but they were too anxious in insisting on our staying. Having been fooled once, we decided that was enough. We suspected there was a Rebel camp near, and that the officer would soon be back with too many men for our small force to resist. So we declined dinner and left just in time. Hardly had we started when the Rebs came down the road, just as we expected, and we had quite a skirmish.

Throughout all this, the citizens became expert in hiding things, and the Yankees equally expert in finding them. At this stage of the campaign, north of Atlanta, we were only occasionally called upon to forage, because we had not yet cut loose from our supply trains as we were to do later in the famous March to the Sea, from Atlanta to Savannah.

Yet even then, if any of the boys while on picket or detached duty saw a fat hen or goose, or a ham hanging handy, or a patch of potatoes, something was mighty apt to stick to his fingers. Many times we cornered a cow and milked her into our canteens.* How some of the supposedly high-toned ladies would talk at us for milking their cows! Other times we robbed bee gums for honey, and oh, how some of the boys would get stung!

Generally, with the ladies, the worse the circumstances they were in, the more bitter they were about "Lincoln's hirelings, Yankee scum, and bluebellied sons of b—s." Some said even worse things.

On the streets of Rome, Georgia, when the Yankees marched through the town and passed under the balcony of a young ladies' seminary, the young ladies emptied slops on their heads. Worse than that, they emptied the contents of their chamber pots on the boys.

The boys, to retaliate, said no one but an abandoned woman would do a thing like that. Abandoned women had no rights that anyone was bound to respect, so they did not respect girls who emptied chamber pots. Many a girl thereupon got spanked on her bare flesh and probably was sorry for what she had done, but undoubtedly was madder than ever. We did not go through Rome ourselves, and I only men-

* Editor's note: The pewter mouth of the standard Union canteen measures only three-fourths of an inch, inside diameter, so these Illinois farm boys proved themselves expert milkers.

tion this story to show how bitter the Southern women were. I never saw or personally knew of a woman being insulted or abused by a Yankee.

Up to the time we left Atlanta, we destroyed no private property and after that, as a rule, only such as had been abandoned. There were times, though, when we were too much put upon and had to make exceptions to the rule. Like when we nearly burned a farmhouse down, shortly after leaving Atlanta.

It was at a little Georgia village called Rough and Ready. Some of the boys, wanting a drink of water, went to a house. We found a well there, but no bucket or rope. We went around to the house door and called for the people inside to pass us out their bucket and rope. No one answered. The house was dark; they wanted us to think they had left or were asleep. We knew better. We knew they were not in bed so soon after Yankees had for the first time entered their town.

Then up come a nigger and told us the man of the house had taken away his bucket and rope, swearing that no d——d Yankee should drink out of his well. We called the man several times more. Then we told him that if he did not produce the bucket in a minute, he would wish he had. Still no answer. So we piled a lot of corn fodder against his kitchen house that was off from the main house, and set fire to it.

In less than three minutes, the man came out of the house, with wife and three or four kids, begging, "Please, Mr. Yankee, don't burn down my house!" He said he was asleep and did not hear us call. The corn stalks soon burned down, and a few buckets of water put out the fire. But I don't believe that man was ever more frightened in this world. We told him we would let him off this time, since he turned civil, but that we had calculated to roast him alive in his own house.

As we went along in the March to the Sea, our orders while out foraging were to capture all Confederate soldiers that we could take, seize all horses and mules, burn all cotton and all Rebel government stores, but to respect all private property except for the forage necessary for man and beast. We were not to molest any citizens who remained at home and did not act as bushwackers. As far as I know, these orders were respected.

Every morning on the march, a detail of men was made up from each of the ten companies of the regiment for foraging. The foragers also acted as scouts for the army, and often picked up such information as would require them to hurry back to the column and report.

Our foraging expeditions ranged from a mile to five or six miles on the flanks of the marching column. Of course, the enemy had troops out to intercept us and capture all such parties. Nearly every day, the foragers had brushes with the enemy cavalry. Some men proved too timid to make good foragers. Others seemed to be specially pleased by the freedom from discipline that they had. By freedom from discipline, I ought to explain that I don't mean that they were licensed to plunder any way at all. It was like this:

The column had to march in four ranks abreast, one man just so close to another, with no turning out

Sherman's Bummers foraging

for mudholes, creeks or anything else; no falling out
for water or anything else, and no straggling, ahead or
behind the column. The forager, on the contrary, left
camp any time he pleased, day or night, just by making his business known to those in command. He
went where he pleased, as he pleased, and could rest
when he pleased. All he had to do was to return to
camp when he got his load. Comparatively speaking,
he had an easy time.   .

   Men who made good foragers were pretty sure to
be detailed for the business, and these men in time
came to be called bummers, because they bummed
everywhere. After we entered South Carolina, they
were made into a regular detail.

   Well, I was very often sent out as a forager and
often volunteered to go for someone who did not feel
well. I don't know whether I went because I hated to
march in line, or because I liked a little more freedom, or because my nose would smell out hidden
forage very well. Anyway, I went.

   We bummers were expected to return to our regiment at night with our loads of provisions. We always
did so unless prevented. Sometimes we would get so
far away from our column as to make it impossible to
return before night. After dark, it was not safe traveling, nor was it easy to find our own troops.

   The bummers of each company were allowed one
mule or one horse on which to bring our forage in.
Each had a rough pack saddle. It was a comical sight
to see our mule. Sometimes he would have a little of
everything on his back: flour, beans, meat, potatoes,
rice, hams, bacon, molasses in jugs, chickens with

their feet tied together and thrown over the mule's neck, and on top of all maybe a pig or sheep or calf with its feet tied—but not its mouth. If the mule was too loaded to carry a calf or sheep, we would tie a rope around its neck and tie the other end to the mule's tail.

As we parties of bummers would approach the column or camp, ten or twenty such mules and horses would appear, and what a sight! If we made a night march and got into camp in early morning, the roosters would crow, the pigs squeal, the sheep bleat, the calves bawl, the mules themselves bray, and the bummers do all four or five of those things, besides singing at the top of their voices, "We Won't Go Home Until Morning." The soldiers would cheer our arrival and rush up for a division of what we brought.

The citizens, on the other hand, soon learned to keep out of sight everything that could be eaten. They would hide or bury everything they had time to put away. But we became expert in hunting. They would bury things in all imaginable places. If we did not find as much as we thought we should, we would institute a search and go all around the yards, prodding into the ground with our bayonets and our iron ramrods.

On one occasion, we came up to a big plantation house and found the people, an old, grey-headed man and his family of women, and a few darkies, gathered in the family graveyard which, according to the custom of the country, was near the house. They informed us that they had just buried one of their dead. We expressed sympathy but explained to the old gentleman how necessary it was for us to obtain forage. So we searched the premises and found next to nothing.

We knew the stuff was hidden, for the darkies kept grinning all the time. It struck us that the family did not express much grief over their dead they had just buried. So after telling them how sorry we were for their loss, etc., we expressed a strong desire to know more about the dear departed whom they had just buried. Neither the man nor the women were very communicative. They just said it was a child.

We finally told them we were determined to dig the body up. The women screamed and begged us not to desecrate the grave. The old man asked us if we thought he had lied to us, and said, "I am a Southern gentleman." He said he hoped we would not outrage the feelings of his ladies and himself. All this time the niggers were grinning and winking at one another when they thought no one saw them. So we ordered the niggers to dig up the body and let us see it. The old man said that if they did, he would flog them. We told them that if they did not, we would shoot them.

The darkies were more afraid of us than they were of their master, just then, so they dug open the grave and uncovered a long box, wide and deep. Right there, the women began to call us thieves and rascals. We made the niggers take the cover off the box, which was seven feet long and four feet wide. It was filled with hams, bacon, meal, flour, etc. We loaded "the dear departed" onto our mules and returned to camp, at which point it truly departed forever.

At another house, we hunted and hunted but could

find nothing. The people all said the Yanks had been there and cleaned them out of everything. As we could not find tracks of man nor beast around the house, we concluded that they were lying, but hunt as we would we could find nothing.

In a field near the house was a nigger working a poor old broken-down mule and another nigger sowing wheat. When we came up, both nigs quit work and stared at us. We were about to give up the hunt when we noticed the niggers were rolling their eyes and grinning. Remembering the fresh "grave," we began to stick our ramrods into the ground. Pretty soon my rod found a soft place. We made the niggers bring a spade and go to digging. There we found more stuff than we wanted.

Sometimes the nigs were loyal to their masters. Then neither coaxing nor threats would induce them to tell where things were hidden.

In foraging we always went up to a house on the run, so if there were any Reb soldiers in it we could surprise them. Once we rushed up to a house and found not a soul there, white or black. But we found the dining room table set with a hot dinner and part of the dinner still on the stove. Evidently the family were surprised just as they were about to eat.

The hot food was too tempting. We quit looking for the people, fed our mules, and sat down to the table and feasted. We told stories, made speeches, drank toasts to the departed ladies of the house, and had a good time. We spent a while over our dinner and had hardly finished when one of the boys, looking outside, said: "Thunder, look here!"

Coming up the lane to the house at a gallop was a squad of Rebel cavalry. We jumped up, grabbed and cocked our guns, and got ready. As they halted, the officer says, "Surround the house and shoot any of them that runs."

We opened fire on them at short range, ordering them to surrender or we would wipe them all out. They gave one look at how many we were, and jumped on their horses and left. We went out and secured the horses of the wounded Rebs, and asked how they knew we were there. At first, they denied knowing anyone was there. On our explaining to them gently and kindly that we were no fools and knew they lied, they said that the inmates of the house had fled to their camp a couple of miles away and begged them to go and rescue their property; that they had been detailed to come and either kill or capture us. They added that we could not escape, for as soon as their comrades returned to camp a larger party would be sent to take us.

We concluded that "he who fights and runs away, may live to fight another day," so we hurriedly loaded our mules. Taking our prisoners, we left for our column and managed to get there without again being disturbed. We turned our prisoners over to headquarters.

It was a good thing for the house and neighborhood where we had the fight that our attackers were plainly Rebel soldiers. We had orders that if our foragers were fired on by citizens, all houses within a certain distance around were to be burned to the ground. The reason for this was that unless some such measures were taken, we would always be in a quarrel with the local citizens. Many of us would be killed, and many more women and children would be killed by the foragers in returning fire at folks who shot at them. The citizens could not hope, by killing a few foragers, to stop our army or even to save their property. It was better if they took things easy. As they had to take their medicine anyway, the best way was to take it quiet.

All the same, a great many foragers and scouts were killed by the citizens. On our approach, usually all the men would run into the woods. By this, I mean old men and boys. If there were but two or three of us foragers, the women would be mighty pleasant to us and do their best to detain us. Meanwhile, if the men in the wood could get up enough strength so they thought it safe, they would return and creep up and fire on the unsuspecting soldiers. They would kill whole small parties of foragers and bury them in the woods. Many a poor Yank has lost his life in this way. Not half of the worst side of it have I told, nor will I tell.

Of course, an attack by Rebel soldiers was legitimate warfare. For attacks by them, we never made retaliation on the citizens. It was a different matter when it came to being shot by bushwhackers. The fulltime bushwhackers did not make much difference between Yank or Reb, but murdered either when they could gain anything by it. They would kill a man for his clothes or for a dollar.

These bushwhackers were citizens of the South, but were too mean-spirited and cowardly to enter the

Rebel Army. So they hid in the brush to escape being drafted, and robbed all people, Rebel and Union alike. And both armies, when they caught bush-whackers, shot them down cold. It was far different with citizens who behaved themselves.

I never but once saw citizens robbed of anything more than something to eat or to wear. That once was when a squad of us went foraging with a captain from another company in charge of us. We came to a house and found plenty of forage. While we were loading our mules, we noticed that this Captain Culver en-gaged in earnest conversation with the owner of the house. The two of them went into the house and soon came out. When we got the mules loaded and were ready to start, the man asked the captain to step into the house again, but the captain did not go.

The man kept urging something of the captain, but he shook his head and finally swore at the man and told him to go away and leave him alone. The man then lost his temper and openly called the captain a "thief and a liar." We stepped up and asked what was the matter. The old gentleman told us that when we first came there, the captain took him into the house and told him that we men were all hard cases and would rob him of everything he had; if he had money or jewelry and wanted to save it, the best way was to give it to the captain to keep until we were ready to go, when the captain would return it to him pri-vately. On the strength of this, the old gentleman said, he had given the captain two gold watches, money, rings, and other jewelry, and now the captain refused to return them.

We turned on the captain and told him we were not thieves even if he was. We gave him his choice: return the property *now* or we would put him under arrest. He finally disgorged until the old gent said that was all. The captain begged us not to report him, and we agreed if he promised he would not steal again. He promised.

Relationships between Union soldiers and southern civilians were sometimes strained, especially with housewives who saw their pantries and smokehouses plucked clean of provisions. The same tactics sometimes worked well in supplying soldiers with items which their own commissary or the quirks of war failed to produce. "If you need it, go and git it," was one of the unwritten rules of warfare.

 # if you can't "pick" rebs, "pick" yanks

AFTER A big day's fight, especially if it was raining, the quartermasters would issue a gill of whiskey to each man. As I did not use or want the whiskey, I would trade it for coffee. Many in the army, however, stood ready to value whiskey above most everything else.

No one was allowed to sell a soldier whiskey, but all the same they could always get it. Even early in the war, when we lay back at Nashville, Tennessee, it was so. There we were about half a mile from the cemetery. By sneaking through the cemetery at night, the boys could reach a sort of private grog shop kept by an old Irish woman.

We had in our company two men who were very fond of "tangle foot." One was the Jimmie McMillan of whom I have written elsewhere. The other was a boy about eighteen years old named Joe. They used to slip past the guard and go to the old Irish woman's shop and fill up. Then they would come back to camp and try to run the camp. Each time, they would be put in the guard house to sober up.

We in camp had just gone to bed one night when Jimmie came in crying like a baby. Some of us got up and tried to put him in his bunk. He refused to go, and kept on crying and repeating: "The Holy Virgin forgive me, but I killed the boy."

We made out from what Jimmie said that he and Joe had been on a drunk and, coming home, had run into trouble. We looked around for Joe but could not find him. Jimmie then said he had not seen Joe since they entered the cemetery on the way back to camp. We took lights and hunted for Joe. Well, we finally found him. He had fallen into an open grave. There was water in the grave, and Joe was both dead drunk and nearly drowned.

I remember one time when our officers had invited officers of the other companies in our regiment to take supper with them, and to have a game of cards that evening as part of the entertainment. They had procured from our quartermaster several canteens full of whiskey.

Some of our boys cut a slit in the back of the tent, where the whiskey canteens were hanging against the rear tent pole. Our boys emptied the whiskey into their own canteens and filled the officers' with water.

When the officers had been playing cards for a while, someone says to the servant, "Dan, bring us a canteen." We who had stolen the whiskey, or who knew about it, gathered around to await developments. Dan brought a canteen. Says one of our officers: "This is the genuine stuff. Try it." So drinks were poured out and put to their lips. "Adam's ale is good but not very strong," says one drinker. So T. S. Rogers, who was then our captain, smelled of the canteen.

"Dan, bring us another canteen, and no fooling," Captain R. ordered. Dan brought another canteen. The captain sniffed and snorted, "What's the matter with you, Dan, did I not tell you to get some whiskey?" Up spoke Dan, " 'Fore de Lawd, Massa Captain, I done got the whiskey and brung it up here. I 'spec the debbil done work a dark miracle." At last, the captain ordered, "Bring all the canteens and let me see." All the canteens were found to contain water. On investigation, they found the slits in the tent. Then Rogers and Scott and the others just raved. None of us boys, of course, knew anything about it. That whiskey inspired in more ways than one.

Along about this time, we were poorly fed. A great number of freight cars loaded with rations were not far away, standing there, so one night the boys organized a raid on the cars. As there were guards on them, we chose a dark, rainy night. Without much trouble, we cut holes through the bottoms of several cars and carried off what was inside.

As we learned later, those cars contained rations for the boys at Atlanta. They were opened the next morning and found empty. About ten that morning, our colonel and adjutant went to every tent. After telling us that certain cars had been found empty, they said that the colonel had received notice to search all tents. The colonel said, "I know my boys would not raid the cars, but if anything from them is found in any of your tents, you will be punished."

After that warning, naturally nothing was found. After the searching party had come and gone, the boys could be seen bringing out of hiding hams and shoulders, crackers, candles, and all sorts of things. And you may be sure that the colonel got his share of the good things. He was a real understanding colonel.

On another occasion when we were in camp, all of us were ordered out on drill except one old man who was left as camp guard. Our sutler or "traveling merchant" got him drunk for the devil of it and then whipped the old man. It made us all mad. That night, we organized a raid on the sutler.

The sutler had his goods in a special tent, the tent held down by guy ropes. We formed in two lines, with each line led by a boy with a knife. I am glad that it is not necessary to say who the leaders were. The leaders with their knives ran ahead and cut the tent ropes. The others followed and quickly stripped the tent of its goods.

Expecting the worst, the sutler had gotten the colonel to furnish him with several guards. These now thoughtfully fired their guns in the air and shouted, "Halt!" Nobody did. The sutler meanwhile ran to the colonel and called him out. It took the colonel an amazingly long time to dress, because usually he could get put together in seconds. At last they came running, with the colonel shouting, long before he could see us, "Disperse, disperse at once to your quarters! If I catch any of you, it will go hard with you." Taking the hint, we dispersed before he got there.

In about a half an hour, the colonel went through the streets of our regimental camp with a guard. In every street, he raved at us and said he would have our quarters searched the next day and did not want to find a thing of the sutler's in any tent. Then he posted a guard over the camp so we could not go out and hide things as we had done after the freight car raid. Unfortunately, the guard could not see very well that night. When the search was made next day, it was thorough but nothing was found. Not long afterwards, the colonel received some mysterious gifts of boxes of cigars, canned meats, and the like. I do not recall that he asked where they came from.

About this time, I encountered the joys of picket duty. I am not joking about picket duty. Nearly all of the boys liked it, as it rid us of camp duty, drilling, and such. While there was some danger to being posted at a distance from the main body, as pickets were, we had more liberty. A picket while off duty could go fishing or swimming, or make a call at some farmhouse inside or near to our lines. In addition to my own turn at picket, I always stood ready to go for another and often did. This way, I got to see right much of the countryside under somewhat pleasanter and friendlier circumstances than whilst foraging.

At that time, everything had to have revenue

stamps on it. A great number of the poor whites in the South, who could not read, would trade bread or something to eat for these stamps. They somewhere got the idea the stamps were money, and we did not go to great pains to disabuse them of it.

The girls on these little farms were always glad to see us and were not at all bashful, but we had to be very careful lest they betray us to the bushwhackers who were always lurking near. The houses mostly contained but two rooms, and each room had from two to three beds in it. Each bed had a kind of curtain called a "valance." The space under the bed was a repository for innumerable things, from dogs to butter bowls, sacks of meal, and potatoes. These things were put under the bed simply to be out of the way, for want of other places for them. We found all sorts of things under there. More than once, we pulled a hiding Johnny Reb out from under the bed.

One woman, I remember, was ready to scald us with her kettle when we began to search under the beds for Rebs. We told her that if she did, we would burn down her house, so she changed her mind.

At the same place, we reached up between the logs of the house, in spaces they used like narrow shelves, and pulled down the girls' splints. These were about ten inches long and an inch wide. When the girls grabbed at them and tried to take them back, we held on to them for the fun of it. At that, the old lady says: "Drat it, what do you want of them? You can't use them. Sal and Sis can't go to preachin' without them."

We had no idea what the splints were for, but pretended we did. Later we found out they were put in

Major General Joseph Hooker

Major General William T. Ward

Fortifications and approach to Kennesaw Mountain, Tennessee

General Kilpatrick and his staff

Union troops guarding a railway bridge

Yankees doing camp chores

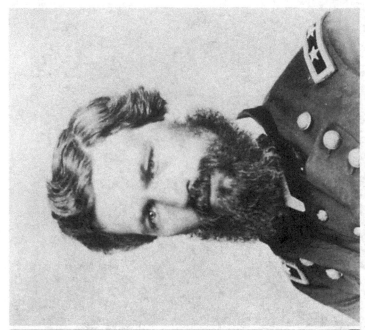

General Oliver Otis Howard

General Henry Warner Slocum

Rebel fortifications and approaches to Atlanta

The city of Atlanta

front of Sunday dresses for stiffening. I suppose they took the place of a corset.

Every house had dogs, some as many as eight or ten dogs, and every dog had any number of fleas. They were measly hounds, constantly scratching. These were, of course, at the houses of the "pore white trash."

The planters' houses were entirely different. Generally, they were large white houses with beautifully-laid-out grounds, semi-tropical trees, and flowers and plants in plenty. A little ways from the house would be the niggers' quarters. Generally these were neat log huts, whitewashed and clean inside and out. A crowd of half-naked picanninies, some of the smallest entirely naked, would be running around the quarters.

The mistress of the house and the young ladies, although hating us cordially, were generally true ladies and so conducted themselves. All the same, their houses were searched for bushwhackers and their smoke houses were made to contribute to our larder. Some were rabid Rebels and took no pains to conceal it, but all were polite to us except when we were searching their houses.

Many times, the ladies would ask us to take up our quarters in their yard for their own safety, and then the girls would play and sing for us, and the darkies would cook for us, and we had a fine time. Sometimes the girls would sing "Dixie," sometimes "The Bonnie Blue Flag," or a song beginning, "If you want to hear Lincoln and Yankeedom swear, just mention the Mason and Slidell affair." We would retaliate by sing-

ing some of our patriotic songs. I had sense enough to
know I could not sing, so I told stories. Nearly always,
before we left such places and returned to camp at the
end of our picket duty, all had become good friends.*

The girls would tell us in what Rebel regiment
their fathers, husbands, brothers were, would sometimes add with a sly look: "Now remember, young
man, tell Jim (or Charley) not to hurt you." We
would reply, "After this, for your sake, we will look
out for Jim (or Charley) and if he falls into our hands
he shall be safe." Then the girls would laugh and say,
"Oh, how kind you are." All the same, I am sure that
each took the others' words for just what they were
worth. I don't suppose they believed a word we said.
Yet some lasting friendships were formed, and some
girls were later wed Union.

Young people everywhere will be young people. If
we stayed in the same place long, the boys would have
their sweethearts and there would be much talk of
"my girl." We got up dances inside our lines and as
the girls had no other escorts but us, they seldom
refused to go with us. Often some old maid would go
along for propriety's sake, or perhaps the mother

* Editor's note: The Mason-Slidell song and incident are almost
forgotten. The incident occurred when a United States warship
intercepted a British mail steamer bearing Messrs. Mason and
Slidell as Confederate emissaries to Great Britain. Both men
were taken prisoner and carried to New York. British indignation soared at this violation of the "freedom of the seas." Britain
almost declared war on the United States. Our government,
which had not authorized the shanghaiing, was greatly embar-
rassed—hence the reference in the song—but apologized and
averted an Anglo-American war.

would let them go with only some darky along, male
or female, to carry a lantern. But generally a number
of girls would go together. So you see, it was not "all
work and no play," although the play spells were few
and far between.

At times, we came across people who were Union-
ist, but were afraid to confess it for fear their neigh-
bors would hear of it. The negroes could and did tell
us who were Union, and they would guide us near to
their hiding places. For some of these people had
made themselves so unpopular locally that they found
it best to get out of the way for a time.

We also got to know the people well by being ordered to special duty as "safe guards." Sometimes the
head of a family, often a woman because the man was
in the Rebel Army, would ask for a safe guard. If on
enquiry no objections were found, the safe guard
would be furnished. His duty was to keep soldiers
from trespassing, and the fact that he was there was
usually enough to keep everything safe. The safe
guard had a soft snap. Nothing in the house was too
good for him. He had a good bed made up for him on
the porch floor, with clean blankets and a *pillow*! He
ate at the family table. As coffee was next to impossible to get in the South, the safe guard would trade
his rations to his comrades for coffee and turn it over
to the cook at the house, and that alone would be
enough to make the ladies pleasant.

At one place in Georgia, I was put on duty as a safe
guard. Among the children there was a little girl four
or five years old and we became great friends. She
would sit on my lap of an evening while I smoked my

pipe, and talk about her papa. She could not help telling me that the Yanks were terrible fellows. Of course, she was too young to know I was a Yankee and her talk amused me. She said her papa had gone to kill the Yankees to keep them from hurting his little girl.

The little girl said that her big sister hated the Yankees, too. As the sister was near, I would laugh and ask the little one what her sister would do if a Yankee were to come there. Would she give him a kiss? "No, sir, she just hates them!" All the same, the sister did kiss a Yankee later on, and married him, too. The boy who took my place as safe guard married her. When we marched on, he left her behind until the close of the war.

Another fellow who married a Southern girl, so I heard, was Daniel Jones. At the start of our campaign, he had a sweetheart back home. He could not read or write, and that is how I knew about the girl back home. All through the campaign, I wrote his letters to her and read her letters to him. Finally he proposed, in a letter he had me write, but she was not prepared to marry so she refused him. After we got into the deep South, I heard he had proposed to a Southern girl, wed her, and left her behind until the war should end. There were many such cases. No doubt many returned or sent for their wives. I don't suppose that they all did, or ever intended to.

There was one thing about Southern girls that chilled me. As far as my knowledge goes, all the women of the lower classes and a good many of the better class used tobacco in the form of snuff. Once while on a scout in Kentucky, I went to a big, fine house for my dinner. While the cook was getting dinner, the young ladies of the house asked us into the parlor, and played and sang for us. After dinner, we returned to the parlor. One of the girls, a pretty and smart one, too, went to the marble mantle and took down a silver tobacco box. She passed it around, the girls helping themselves. I did not chew then, and it disgusted me, but I soon got used to such sights.

As we went through Georgia, we often had an opportunity to read in the newspapers how terrible we were. We found these papers in houses. They were queer reading to us. They would state that the arch-fiend Sherman, with his horde of Lincoln hell-hounds, had come as far as they would ever get; that "General Johnston has been driving them into a trap and is about ready to spring the trap"; and when he does, "not one of the invaders will be left alive to tell the tale." They would assure the people of some village or city that Sherman was within forty or fifty miles, but never fear, he could never reach them.

As we neared the city of Milledgeville, which was the capitol of the state of Georgia then, the papers that we found just plain raved. Some warned Sherman that "his end was near." They said the proud state of Georgia never would submit to having her state house desecrated by vandals. "Should she see her proud and beautiful seat of government laid waste? No, never!" Sooner that every son of the state would lay down his life and the women would take up arms

and repel the scum of the North, the vile abolition-
ists. "Whilst a man or woman remains alive, no vile
Yankee shall set foot in our state capitol."

The papers reported that the legislature was in session devising means of keeping us out. Troops were
being massed in our front to annihilate us. Of course,
the papers' bluster and threats only made us laugh.
More than that, when the time came the bummers
alone captured the city of Milledgeville with but a
few shots. The legislature stuck to their work until we
were within a few miles, then fled with the state
papers.

While we were in the city, we visited the legislative
hall, which stood vacant. We elected a governor,
speaker, and members, and transacted regular legislative business. We passed laws and resolutions con-
demning the South for its barbarous manner of
treating prisoners, voted ourselves big pay for our
two-day session, and altogether those halls heard more
fun and sense than they ever had before.

The different regiments had men of every occupa-
tion, so each got busy in his way. Some printers took
possession of a printing office and got out a news-
paper. Others, the pious ones, hunted up ministers
and deacons and talked with them of the evil of their
ways and quoted scripture to them to prove them in
the wrong. We made game of everybody and everything, but no private property was destroyed.

Some of us who went foraging in Milledgeville saw
a yellow flag floating in front of a house. One says,
"Smallpox!" I says, "I never had the smallpox but I
am going in to get it." Some of the others went with

Union troops raise the flag atop the Governor's house—
Milledgeville, Georgia

The Capitol at Milledgeville, Georgia

me to the door. The door was opened by a nigger. Behind him were two or three ladies. "Have you had the disease?" says a lady. "No, but we want it," says Hank Hoffman. "We are coming in, and if the patient is bad, we will take him to the hospital."

"The patient is a woman," says the lady, "and I am sure you have not the convenience for taking care of her that we have." But we persisted, "By your leave, we will see the patient." Then the lady got mad and began to sputter. The nigs began to grin and roll their eyes, and we were surer than ever that there was no smallpox there. The yellow flag had been put up just to scare away the Yanks. The boys walked in, filled their haversacks, and advised the woman to put up *two* flags next time.

Disease and lack of sanitation killed nearly three times as many soldiers as bullets. Measles, pneumonia and dysentery were among the great slayers. Like most soldiers on both sides, Bob Strong eventually landed in an Army hospital. He collapsed near Marietta, not far from Atlanta, and was sent back to a base hospital at Chattanooga.

what an army hospital was like

ABOUT THE sixth day of July, 1864, I got so bad with rheumatism and dysentery that I could not walk. I went and lay down under the doctor's tent. We were then near Marietta. On the morning that the regiment marched on to Marietta, I was a little in the rear when the bugles sounded. "Fall in!" I picked up my gun and started to go to the regiment. When I got part way, I fell down beside a tree.

The colonel passed and saw me. He asked what I was doing there and why I was not in a hospital. I told him I did not want to go to the hospital, so had started for the regiment. He ordered me to stay where I was while he sent for our doctor. Before he came, Doctor Beggs, who belonged to us but had been detailed to a New Jersey regiment, came along, saw me, and had me taken by ambulance to the division hospital in the rear. This was a temporary tent affair.

That night, the boys came to see me. They said the colonel just raised h—— with our doctor for not taking better care of the boys, and asked why he had not sent me to the hospital where I belonged.

After the Battle of Marietta, the hospital soon filled with wounded and sick. The hospital doctor came through to decide who among us should be sent farther to the rear. No real soldier wanted to go to the hospital. We were all lying on the ground, so as soon as I saw the doctor coming, I sat up. I tried to make him think I was able to go to the front, but he ordered me to get ready to go back to Chattanooga. It did not take me long to get ready, as my wardrobe was all on my back and feet.

When the ambulance came for us, we were taken to the railroad cars. These were cattle cars, with a little straw on the bottom. We had to pack close to get into them. None of us were able to stand or sit up many minutes at a time and the hospital men who were with us to help us could not do much for us except bring water.

So many trains were rushing to the front with rations and ammunition that our progress was slow. We took three days getting to Chattanooga. While on the train, I traded coffee and sugar—I had been too sick to eat for a long time and had several pounds of each—for blackberries. I got my haversack, cup, and cap full. I ate them all and traded for more. In those three days I think I ate a bushel of berries, and I have always believed that they saved my life.

Ambulances met the train at Chattanooga and took us to the hospital. Each man had a narrow cot with a clean sheet. The first thing I remember in the hospital was sitting up on my cot and pulling my shirt over my head. The male nurse spoke pleasantly to me, and said I had better keep my shirt on. He told me afterwards that I had been crazy for three days and that if I had not been so weak they would have had to tie me down. Said I had eaten nothing since I arrived there.

The nurse then asked my name, company and regiment; what state I was from; my father's and mother's names and where they lived. He wrote it all down on a piece of paper and fastened it to the head of my bed. I asked him, "What's all that for?" and he said, so that if I died, they could notify my regiment and my people. I remember telling him I did not propose to die yet. He laughed and said, "So?" and nothing more.

Everyone was very kind and good to the very sick who were expected to get well, but those who seemed nearly dead had little attention paid to them except to see that they received what they needed. There had been a big battle at the front and soon the wounded were brought in.

After my talk with the nurse, the next thing I remember is seeing a young and handsome boy, who lay next to me on the right, keep picking at his fingers and then at his nose. I spoke to him, but he paid no attention to me. Soon the doctor came, examined me, added a little to the card the nurse had put up, and then went to the boy.

I then learned why the boy did not answer me. He

did not know anything. He had been shot clear through the head, the ball entering just under the eye and coming out at the back of his head. The doctor took a silk rag, oiled it, threaded it into a long silver needle, and pushed the needle clear through the boy's head. He drew the silk rag after it and brought out three or four great big maggots. He repeated this several times, all the while talking soothingly to the boy. Then he dressed the wound and gave the boy something to quiet his nerves.

The next man had been shot through the body. The doctor with his probe went into the wound, cleaned it, pushed some cotton into the wound to keep it open, and went on.

By this time I was sick of it. My stomach had nothing in it, or it would have come up. Before this, I had seen men killed by the hundred and cut to pieces by shells. But I had never seen a doctor cut a man up. I surely did while I was there.

At the end of our tent, separated from us only by a flap of cloth, was the amputating room. I, being near the end, could hear and see nearly everything done there.

As soon as possible, they placed men from the same commands together. In a few days they put near me two of my regiment, one wounded in the leg and the other in the arm. Both had to have their limbs amputated. First they took to the table a boy from near Downer's Grove named Depew or something like it. They carried Depew over while the others were asleep. They took his wounded arm off and took him back. He never opened his mouth during the operation, but he looked mighty pale when they brought him back. As soon as they laid him on his cot, he grasped my hand with the one he had left, but he did not cry.

When they took the other man out, he began to curse and cry. All the chloroform they gave him did not quiet his tongue, and he kept yelling and cursing and crying, "Oh!" all the time that they were cutting off his leg, even though the choloroform held his leg still.

In a few days, both the amputees and the boy with the hole through his head were sent to Nashville, as that place was farther from the front and all hospitals here were filled up again as fast as they were emptied. Two kinds of patients stayed—those who could not recover, and those who would soon be ready to go back to duty at the front.

As soon as I was able, I wrote to you people and also to the boys in the regiment. Got someone else to address the letters. Pretty soon, your letters which came to the regiment after I left for the hospital were sent to me. Among them were ones from Mother and from sister Mary, the last of which was mostly about how our poor brother Albert was bound to enlist. I remember I was just weak enough to cry over each letter, and that I put them under my head for safekeeping.

During this time, our hospital food was what we called soft diet. It consisted mostly of soups and soft bread with butter, jellies, jams. As we grew stronger, they gave us mashed potatoes and a small piece of beef steak. Each boy's meal was brought to him on a tray and set on his bed. If he was too weak to feed himself, he was fed and coaxed to eat. Some had a ravenous appetite which had almost to be choked off. Others wanted nothing. The nurses would coax them, "Eat a little so you'll be able to go home on furlough."

When I got well enough to go outdoors, I had my first good chance to see the outside of a big army hospital. I found the hospital was laid off in streets. Each street was numbered, and every eight or ten tents were called a ward. I was in Ward B, I forget the street number.

In the adjoining tent were some desperately wounded men. One day the sergeant in charge of our ward asked me to go to the next tent with him to see them dress the wounds of a certain badly wounded man. This man was hit in the left side. The shell had cut away a portion of his side, ribs and all. When his wound was exposed for dressing, one could see his heart beat. I did not learn whether he ever recovered, but they were doing their best for him.

Another fellow in the same tent was badly wounded but in a very awkward way. He had lost so big a piece of flesh, behind, that he could not sit down. If he recovered, a bustle would become him.

Eighteen or twenty rods from my tent, and just in front of it, was the "Dead House." All bodies were taken directly from the wards to the Dead House, and if not claimed and removed by friends, they were cut up. There were always many citizen doctors present there from pure patriotism and for the chance they had of dissecting the dead. All remains were supposed to be given honorable burial after dissection, but I suppose those in charge of the burials found their sad work confusing. Sometimes, I know, they did not do their job. The hospital privies were next to the Dead House. Many times, I have seen the intestines of dead men in the vault. More than once, I have seen the intestines hanging from the seats, not having been pushed in properly. It was horrible, but we got used to it. And all the while, we knew we would be misused the same way if we died. A live man was taken care of, but a dead man was no good except to experiment with.

The Christian Commission used to furnish us men with Testaments and tracts and a sort of thread-and-needle case with pockets, called a "housewife." These were made by Northern women and girls, and not infrequently contained letters. One that I got before being sent to the hospital contained a letter from a girl who said she was thirteen years old. She asked the soldier who got her "housewife" to correspond with her, and added that her father and one brother were in such-and-such a regiment. I did write her, and while I was in the hospital she wrote back, saying that in a recent battle her father had been killed and her brother wounded. She asked me to look for her brother in the hospital. I made many inquiries but never heard of him.

As soon as I felt better, I began to bother the doctor to have me sent to the front. He refused steadily for a while. Finally he told me that there was a drove of cattle to be sent to the front, and if I could ride a horse I could go with them. So I started out, rode for two days, was taken worse, and sent back to the hospital. The doctor laughed and said he knew I would be back, but thought he would satisfy me that he knew more than I did. So he let me try it.

It was at this time that I heard that Atlanta finally had been captured. The Rebel General Hood had relieved the Rebel General Johnston, and our boys had a big battle with him, called the battle of Peachtree Creek, on July 20th. Our boys had only one line and no breastworks. The Rebs charged with four lines. Our boys actually ran over them, so I was told when I later returned to my regiment. With the fighting over, the army rested and prepared for what was to come.

As the doctor still refused to send me to the front, I wrote to Scott, who had command of the company, that I was coming. To help me along the way, I wrote cousin Henry Strong, whose regiment was doing garrison duty between Chattanooga and the front, that I would visit him such-and-such a day. I then walked out of the hospital, went to the armory where my gun and accoutrements had been stacked with others, and selected my gun and belts, etc. Next I went to the railroad depot and mingled with the soldiers who were to go down on the next train as guards. I mounted with them on the top of a car, and rode to Henry's camp. There I got off and inquired for him. He was the brigade blacksmith, and I had no trouble finding him. He was in his tent, playing poker, with a pile of money laying before him. I stayed with him that night, and the next day got on a freight train.

So far, so good, but after I got on the freight train I found it did not stop at the Chattahoochee River where my regiment was. I had a choice of stopping ten miles this side of camp and walking on, or going to Atlanta and walking back nine miles. On top of that, I had no money to buy food. Anyhow, I concluded to stop this side and walk the ten miles. That way, I would be walking downhill. If I went on to Atlanta, I would have to walk the nine miles uphill. The engineer advised me not to get off in the country. He said the Rebs frequently raided the railroad line, and if they caught me, it was "Goodbye Yank!"

I got off the train as planned, anyhow, and fell in behind it, keeping a sharp lookout. At one place, a company of cavalry rode up to the top of the railroad cut I was in. They saw me before I could hide. Presenting their guns, they yelled for me to come up and surrender. Being alone, I had no alternative but to obey them. Fortunately, they were of my kind, Yankees. After calling me a fool for my risks, they rode off and left me to continue my lonely walk along the tracks.

After a little, I saw some men cross the track. This time I hid in time, crawling into some bushes. I kept crawling toward the men until I could see that they wore the blue. Then I recognized the company. Behold, it was Cal Richert and other comrades of mine! They were out on picket duty. My tramp was over. The boys were all glad to see me. It makes me feel good yet, to remember how well they treated me. They said they never expected to see me again, as the doctor said, "He will never get well!"

The number of generals slain in the Civil War was phenomenally high. Part of the mortality was due to their recklessness in leading frontal attacks on well fortified enemy forces. Now and again, as Bob Strong here admits, there was a tendency to pick off the unpopular generals on one's own side.

 ## discipline makes war hell

WE HAD inspection of arms every Sunday unless we were in battle. None were excused except such as had just come off picket or skirmish line. Our clothes had to be neat and tidy, our brass belt buckles and other brass polished until they shone.

The inspection officer wore white gloves. He would take the iron ramrod of each man's gun, drop it down into the gun, twirl it around, pull it out, and draw it through his white gloves. If it soiled them, he reported us for uncleanliness.*

* Editor's note: This apparently was to guard against an accumulation of unburnt powder and fouling inside the musket at the breech. Such an accumulation could either prevent the musket from discharging, if damp, or, if dry, burn like charcoal—which black powder partly is—and cause a premature discharge while loading. A discharge of this sort could wound or kill the soldier loading.

You must understand that a private has no rights that an officer is bound to respect, and the officer if he sees fit can be a regular tyrant. It all depended on the officer, whether he was a human being or not.

At times during marches, we were not even allowed to straggle from the lines to fill our canteens without permission—and sometimes when we were in a great hurry to go into battle or get somewhere, permission never was given. Different officers handled this different ways.

Once when we were very thirsty, I just went ahead to a house and filled a lot of canteens for myself and comrades. When I returned, Put Scott, who then commanded the company, felt obliged to see me. He waited until I had distributed the canteens. Then he ordered a corporal to arrest me. Corporal Morris Town came to me and placed me under arrest for disobedience of orders.

My regular place was at the head of the company, I being the tallest man but two. I was just behind Scott. As no man under arrest was obliged to do any work, I instantly threw my gun and cartridge box on the ground. Remember, we were paused on a long, long march. "Lieutenant," says Town to Scott, "What about his accoutrements? I can't carry them." Scott says, "Does he refuse to carry them?" Town says, "Can't make a man under arrest carry a gun." So, "Turn him loose," says Scott. All in all, I was under arrest not more than three minutes.

Scott was as bad as the rest of us about doing what was sensible even if it was not military, but he had to arrest us if we disobeyed orders. Then he always turned around and helped us out. We had in the company and regiment a splendid and kindly set of officers. But we thought Put Scott was the kindest of all. He would divide his last cracker or last water in his canteen with the boys. Part of his kindness, perhaps, might have been policy. If he got out of water, he would pass down the lines, shaking the canteens until he found one with water in it. Then he would take a drink.

Scott also was as careless a man as I ever saw. When we would stop to rest on a march, he would unbuckle his sword belt. Many a time when the bugle called, he would march off and leave his sword on the ground. Some of the boys would pick it up, and when Put would miss it and begin to fume, it would be returned to him. It was said that he once left his false teeth, after cleaning them, and someone carried them all day before returning them to him.

Frequently on long marches, the colonel or lieutenant colonel or major or doctor, who were all the mounted officers that an infantry regiment like ours had, would ride back along the line. If they saw some poor fellow who looked sick and worn out, or who was hobbling along on sore feet, they would call him out of the ranks, dismount, and put the lame boy on their horse as a treat to him.

Not all officers were as nice as ours, though, and time and again we had run-ins with others who wanted to be tyrants and bullies over us. Our own officers knew we would not take it, and the others usually found out quick enough.

Once after being on picket all night, we came into

camp just as most of the troops were already in motion. Our regiment had the rear guard and of course would be the last to move out of camp, but we had just enough time to eat. Our lieutenant told us to hurry and eat, so we raked the fire together, boiled our coffee, fried our meat, and ate quick.

Before we had finished our breakfast, along on horseback came a Colonel Asthmulton, who caused us trouble more than once. He wanted to know what we were doing, sitting around eating? And began to curse and swear at us. We told him, and he cursed us all the more. Then he jumped or rode his horse over our pot and frying pans, spilling everything and filling our coffee pot with dirt. Just remember, too, he belonged to another division and had no authority over us. Well, we gathered up our traps without a word, shouldered our guns, and started on. He, having reined in his horse, was cursing us the whole time.

When we got halfway to the regiment, Colonel Asthmulton drew his sword and swore that if we did not double-quick run he would strike us. There were two of us, and we jumped him. We pulled him off his horse, rolled him in the dirt, kicked and cuffed him, and started his horse off without him. Next we told him that if he ever interfered with us again, we would shoot him.

While he was clawing the dirt out of his eyes and brushing off his clothes, we ran. We soon caught up with our company and fell into our places. We told the boys whom we had thumped, a colonel, no less, and to hide us if he came along. Pretty soon he came, his nose bleeding, his eyes swelled. He was swearing as only he could swear. He says to our company, "Boys, did you see a couple of boys running by?" Up answered someone, "Yes, and they were running as if the devil was after them." So the colonel kept on his way, enquiring all the way for two boys, and they were always just ahead.

We had more trouble later on with this same colonel and the general to whom he was chief of staff, Major General Geary of Pennsylvania.*

Part of the trouble between the general and us was the difference between Western and Eastern troops. They, the Easterners, would stand for more than we would. The Second Division of our 20th Corps (we were of the Third Division, all Westerners from Illinois, Indiana, and Ohio) was made up in part of Eastern troops commanded by General Geary. Like us, they wore the corps badge, a white star. General Geary was a martinet, much stiffer with his boys than we of the West could stand.

Geary frequently used to threaten to arrest us when he came across us away from our commanders, foraging, and did often take our forage. Consequently, no one liked him. He was cruel, too, in exacting full discipline of his men. I have many times on the march passed his camp and seen men with a cord tied around their thumbs, standing on tiptoe with their arms stretched above their heads and their thumbs

* Editor's note: John W. Geary, Territorial Governor of Kansas before the Civil War and twice Governor of Pennsylvania after the war. He was noted as an administrator, but even his kindlier biographers mention his temper.

tied to the limb of a tree. It was an ugly sight, and more than once our boys cut the men down.

Also, I have seen men of this division and of the First Division (another Eastern unit) with their hands tied together and drawn down over their knees and with a gag in their mouth. In this helpless position, they eventually tumbled over on one side, lying in the hot sun with flies over their faces, or in the rain and mud. I never saw a Western man used that way, and I honestly believe that if one of our officers had used his men that way, he would have been killed during the first battle thereafter. I have no doubt that many officers were so killed by their own men.

After the war, when I moved and settled in Nebraska, I knew a family of seven brothers from Pennsylvania who were all in the army, although not all in the same regiment. One of them told me that he had shot at General Geary more than once. Another told me that he put a bullet through the carriage that Geary and his adjutant were riding by in. Later in our campaign, when we were marching through North Carolina, I had a tussle or two with Geary myself. I will tell you about that now.

I told you how overbearing Geary was, and how he used to tie up his men by the thumbs and buck-and-gag them, and how his chief of staff, Colonel Asthmulton, was as bad as he and how a couple of us beat up Asthmulton.

Well, the beating we gave Asthmulton made him mad at our brigade. Of course, he knew what brigade we belonged to by the color of the star on our hats, and he and Geary were, if possible, worse to us than ever.

This one time our brigade had been at the rear of the column, and had marched all day and all night. We overtook the advance at daybreak, just in time to get our breakfast and take over the advance, which was the easiest place to march. But we had no time for delay.

When we halted, someone went back to hurry up our company mule, which had our pots and kettles on his back. The man leading the mule was Jerry Wallace, a big fellow. Just as he came up to us, along came General Geary and his staff and ordered Wallace to take his d—n-d mule out of the way. Wallace made a run for it and had nearly got the mule to our position on the side of the road when Geary, with an oath, drew his sword and struck Wallace with the flat of it.

Wallace made one jump like a wildcat at Geary on his horse. Before Geary's staff could help him, Wallace had pulled him from his horse, pounded and kicked him, and had run off into the crowd of us. We during the melee had seized the mule, dragged him to our position, and were unloading him. When Wallace ran in amongst us, the crowd of us closed up around him so that Geary's staff could not follow him.

Geary picked himself up from the dirt and demanded to know who we were. We told him. He said he would find Wallace and have him shot. But Geary kept away from us for a few days, and I suppose he thought better of it, as nothing came of it.

All this helped to make him madder at our brigade,

however, and especially our regiment. One day, our regiment had the advance. We were marching "rear in front," an arrangement which put us of Company B in the extreme advance with the rest behind us.

We in the extreme advance found a plantation with plenty of forage, so we piled a lot of meal and meat by the roadside and left a man to guard it, as we always did in such cases. But we could do no more, for we were in sight of the enemy. In front of us we could see the enemy falling back, and we needed all our men. Mark Naper, who had charge of us, told me to walk back until I met the rest of the regiment and have them send men to guard the stuff. Then the man guarding it and I were to rejoin the extreme advance.

So I started back. The countryside was hilly. Sometimes I could see the rest coming along and sometimes I couldn't. Right in the road, about halfway, I met Geary and Asthmulton. I saluted and stepped aside to let them pass. Geary saw the star on my cap, and it acted on him as a red rag does to a bull. He halted his horse and demanded: "What in hell and damnation are you doing here?" I told him. "You're a d—n-d liar, you are skulking," he says. "About face and go with us until we meet your command."

Calmly as I could, I told him he was mistaken, that I was already obeying orders and could not obey him. He swore I was a liar, and said he would cut me down. With that, he drew his sword. I cocked my gun and told him to put up his sword, or I would shoot him on the spot. Asthmulton meanwhile had made a move to draw a pistol. I shouted, "Stop. Draw that pistol and I'll kill you both where you are!"

I then repeated my story, begged their pardon for my conduct, and explained I could do nothing else. Geary cooled down, and says to Asthmulton, "I expect we were too fast." I then told them where I belonged and that they could enquire there and easily find out whether I was skulking. So Geary says, "I believe you, and I am sorry for my anger."

He went his way and I went the other way. I would certainly have shot one, and perhaps both, if they had struck me with their swords.

All this amounts to nothing now, and I tell it only to illustrate one phase of army life, which had many sides, some good, some bad, some bitter, some sweet, some wet, and some dry.

Earlier in the war, we had trouble of another sort with another high-ranking officer. This was Colonel Benjamin Harrison, later the general commanding our brigade.* I expect he meant well, but it didn't quite work out that way.

At this point, we were still back in Tennessee, not far from Chattanooga. The road we were on was cut up by Buell's and Bragg's armies until just about impassable. Harrison found a guide who said he could take us through the mountains by a nearer and better road. So we marched off on a side road running nearly parallel to the big road, but more to the left. As we went on, the road became dimmer and dimmer, and finally became impossible for our wagons and artillery. So Harrison sent them back all the way to the

---

* Editor's note: The General Harrison who later became President of the United States.

forks of the big road, with a strong guard. He sent all
the horses back. Then he put the guide under arrest.
The guide was undoubtedly leading us into ambush.

After all that, we left the road, such as it was, and
plunged into the woods on our right in an attempt to
cut 'cross country and find the main road. Oh, my
countrymen, what a journey that was! There was not
even a sign of a path. Our way was impeded by rocks
and fallen trees. In places we had to climb or jump as
much as eight feet. In the steeper and longer places,
one of us would help another down. Our clothes were
torn, and so were our hands. It was about three miles
from the foot of the mountains to the main road, and
it took us four hours to make the journey. We called
our trail "Harrison's Pass."

When we arrived at Wauhatchie Valley, near Chattanooga, Harrison went home on a visit to Indiana.
And that set off something else with him. The Eastern troops, opposing General Lee and the Army of
Northern Virginia, always had a camp guard. We
troops of the West seldom set a camp guard when we
had a strong picket out. As long as the boys were in
camp at drill and rollcall, they were allowed at other
times to go where they pleased.

Well, when Harrison returned from his visit home
to Indiana, he took a carriage at Chattanooga and
drove out to camp at night. The camp arrangement
had been changed after he left, and he could not find
his headquarters. So he aroused the inmates of some
tent and had to enquire his way. He finally arrived,
mad as a wet hen.

The next morning, his bugle sang out, "Officer's

call." He assembled all the officers in the brigade and censured them. Next he ordered a camp guard over every regiment, with strict orders to allow no one outside their regimental grounds after "tattoo" or "lights out" at nine P.M. Of course, this was not expected to apply to officers but only to the men and citizens. In the order, though, no such distinction was made.

We were all mad, and agreed amongst us that no one without the password and a written pass from the colonel should go out. I, among others, was put on the first guard detail. We had one guard post, called a gate, where everyone was supposed to go in and out at night. Commonly we let people out anywhere in the daytime, and our particular comrades knew that they could pass in or out at any time of day or night.

Well, when we had been on guard an hour or two under the new orders, an officer tried to pass out of the lines. He had to go to the gate and that made him mad. We kept it up all day, enforcing the orders strictly. I was off duty during the day, but heard it all.

I had just taken up my post that night when I saw the major coming. He approached me. I halted him. "Halt, can't pass here," says I. "I am Major Brown," he says, coming nearer. "I want to go over there to the next regiment." And he started ahead. I leveled my gun and halted him again. "D——n it, Strong, what do you mean by this?" he yelled. "You have to go through the gate, and only through the gate," says I.

The major wouldn't believe it. He went up and down the lines, and tried to pass every guard. Finally he got around to the gate. There the guard halted him with, "Who goes there?" "Major Brown," he replied and kept on without halting. "Halt!" called the guard, bringing his gun to bear.

The major was so mad he just jumped up and down, but he halted and said, "I want to go outside." Says the sentinel, "Advance and give the countersign." "D——n, it, I ha'int got any," says the major. Then the guard sings out, "Corporal of the Guard, to Post Number One!" keeping his gun aimed at the major all the while.

Pretty soon, the corporal comes to see what is the matter. "What is going on, Post Number One?" Says the guard, "Someone wants to pass out and has not got the countersign." Says the corporal to the major, "Have to get the countersign from the colonel." So the major trots off to the colonel and gets the password and returns.

This time the major advances until the guard calls, "Halt, who goes there?" Back he says, "Major Brown with the countersign." "Advance and give the countersign," says the guard, with his bayonet pointing close at Major Brown's heart. The major gives the word and starts by. But the guard halts him again and calls for a written pass. Major has no written pass, makes the night blue with cursing. Guard formally arrests major and sings out again, "Corporal of the Guard, Post Number One." Corporal inquires cause of call. Guard tells him he has arrested a man who has the password, but no written pass. Major Brown now swears like a trooper, with all in earshot stopping to listen. Says the boys all know him, and the guard might as well let him pass.

Corporal looks at Major Brown like he never saw

him before, and says: "You must have a written pass to get out of here, and then be back before midnight." Brown swears, goes to Colonel Harrison, gets a written pass, comes back. Halted again by guard, who summons corporal.

Again corporal arrives, but has no light to read pass. Says he, "If you want me to read your pass, you'll have to fetch a light." Major Brown, mad enough by now to bite nails, gets a light and about an hour after he started to leave camp, finally gets out.

The same thing went on several times during the night. The next morning, the camp guard is taken off by order of Colonel Harrison and we hear no more of it.

I suppose Colonel Harrison came to be pretty well thought of, for he got to be a general, but there was a time when we admired his horse more. We used to say that horse had sense. He was one horse that was afraid of being shot. If the enemy artillery began firing at us while we were behind entrenchments, the horse would jump into the ditch among the boys and try to hide himself. We could always tell when to expect it. The horse would begin to fence sideways. Then with a rush he would be among us. He seemed to know that he was safer in the ditch than out of it. Nothing could hold him when he bolted. I guess there were times when our colonel owed his life entirely to that horse's skittishness under fire.

Officers were not the only ones we sometimes put in their places when we had to. Sergeants got their share of it too, as often happened on picket.

While on picket, non-commissioned officers were

not obliged to stand a turn under arms. They could sleep all night unless called by the sentinel when he had a problem or had to go relieve himself. Most of them, though, counted themselves as going on guard, thus giving the boys off-duty more time to sleep. Often, if we had a good many men on guard, each would have to stand only one trick. All slept near the man on guard, and when his trick was over he would wake the next man, and so on until morning. This applied only when just one man at a time stood sentinel.

There was once sent on guard with us a.sergeant from another company who refused to stand his trick. He said he did not have to, being a sergeant, and be hanged if he was going to lose any sleep. We were to stay out on guard forty-eight hours, so we concluded we would give this sergeant a lesson.

The sergeant had just laid down for a good, long night's rest when a sentinel sings out, "Sergeant, Guard Number One." Up jumps the sergeant and runs to the guard. It was part of a sergeant's job to relieve each man who had necessary business. When the sergeant again laid down, Guard Number Two called him. And so we kept it up all night. Each relief guard as it went on duty was sure to have a sudden epidemic of diarrhea. The sergeant was no fool. Next morning he acknowledged himself beaten and agreed to take his turn on guard.

Al Wiant was on picket one night and had the post at or near the reserve guard. We had officers whose duty it was to visit the picket line day and night to see that the pickets were alert. In the daytime the officer

was called the Officer of the Day. At night he always
was accompanied by one soldier and was called Grand
Rounds.

After the Grand Rounds had been halted and had
announced himself, the sentinel would sing out, "Sergeant, turn out the guard, the Grand Rounds are
coming." At this, the reserve guards would get their
guns, turn out, and stand in line.

Well, that night when the Grand Rounds approached Wiant, just as Wiant called out "halt!" the
Grand Rounds stumbled and fell into some black-
berry bushes. He yelled "Jesus Christ!" Quick as a
flash, Wiant called out, "Sergeant, turn out the
Twelve Apostles, Jesus Christ is coming."

If it rained very hard while on guard or picket, we
would build up a pile of rails, lay some more rails
slanting against the pile with their bottom ends in the
mud, and lie down on the slanting rails to rest with
our rubber blankets pulled over us to keep the rain
off. We were all right unless our knees weakened and
gave out. Then down we would slide, into the mud
and slush. We built such a place in Georgia once and
were on duty all that day and night, only a little way
from the Rebels. Oh, how it rained! The mud was
half knee-deep, we were wet through to the skin, and
didn't dare to build a fire or make any noise.

Our orders were to halt any living thing moving in
our front. Just as morning began to get gray, I saw
out in our front a man slipping along from tree to
tree, followed by one or two more. Apparently they
didn't try to hide from us. The man in the lead

passed post after post until he came to mine. My comrades were asleep.

I took a good look at the man as he came along. He had on an old slouch hat, pulled well down over his face to keep the rain off; wore a rubber blanket, high boots with spurs; and had a sword hanging at his side.

Well, I says to myself, it is Sherman, but he must come in like anybody else. As he got in front of me, I called to halt him. At first he paid no attention, so I cocked my gun and says, "Halt! Come in or I'll fire." They came in, all of them, with their hands out and palms toward me. My halting them woke up the boys and all stood at their guns. Sherman came up, shook hands with us all, and said we were the only post except one to halt him, and that the other post let him go as soon as they knew him. He asked me why I did not let him pass. "Our orders were to halt everything that moved in our front," I said. "You did right," Sherman said. He sat there a few minutes on our rail pile, explained that he was out examining the lines, and left. We saluted him, and he and his companions returned the salute before they left.

One time not long afterward, while we were in battle, Sherman rode up with his staff and dismounted to look through his glass at the Rebel lines. His staff told him to seek cover behind a tree. Instead, he sat down against a tree but with his face toward the enemy, saying: "I guess I can stand anything the boys can." I once saw him lay his hand on a cannon that was firing at the enemy and say to the gunner, "I would rather be a gunner of this battery than to be a major general of the Rebel Army." At any time on marching by him or his headquarters, the boys would give three cheers for "Old Tecump" or for "Billy T," and he would grin and wave his hat to us. Unlike some others, he was a nice general.

On the march, it was a frequent thing for some officer to come riding along, and they always compelled us foot soldiers to quit the road for them, no matter how muddy it was. If the column had halted and the men had laid down to rest, these officers never took any pains to avoid disturbing us. They would make us jump up and get out of their way. But I have known Sherman to order his staff to let down fences by the side of the road, and turn out of the road himself with his staff, rather than disturb "the boys." He never to my knowledge forced any of us to give him the road.

The smaller officers who made us jump aside were only following their natural disposition. You see the same thing in ordinary life. A little property, a little power, better success in life, would make such people too proud to speak to a former associate. Human nature was the same in the army as out of it. A man who was overbearing and domineering at home was the same way in the army. We see it even among children.

*After the fall of Atlanta, the nature of the campaign changed.
Instead of moving in strong concentration along a narrow
route, Sherman's army spread into parallel columns sweeping
and devastating the land. Two things made this possible:
First, a substitution of Confederate generals, John B. Hood
for J. E. Johnston, with Hood marching the main Confederate army north into Tennessee to "suck back" Sherman after
him. Secondly, Sherman's decision to ignore Hood, cut loose
from his base, and head for Savannah in the "March to the
Sea."*

 ## we march from atlanta to the sea

THE REGIMENT and the whole army were now making
preparations for Sherman's great raid or march. We
became convinced that we were going somewhere, no
one knew where. Some guessed one place, some another. The most general guess was Baton Rouge,
Louisiana, where there was reported to be a large
Rebel Army. Others thought we were going to An-
dersonville to release the prisoners held there.

First, we attended to Atlanta. Sherman forced all
prominent citizens to leave and move south. There
were large Confederate government works in Atlanta,

with stores of the munitions of war—shot, shells, uniforms, and so on. All were destroyed, along with all other public property in the city. Then we sent back to the rear all invalids and all our extra stores, extra wagons, extra munitions. After all these were sent back, we received orders to destroy the railroad track north and we did it well. This cut us off from receiving reinforcements and supplies by rail, but it also shielded our rear from Rebels who might move down the same railroad.

The Rebel General John B. Hood was somewhere north and west of us, we knew, saying he was going to recapture Nashville, Tennessee, and then strike for Louisville, Kentucky. As he announced all this in a speech that was printed in the Rebel newspapers, it was hardly a secret to anyone. He must have expected to draw Sherman after him, and turn and attack us at his convenience. If so, he surely got fooled.

General Sherman sent General George H. Thomas with one or two corps, to take care of Hood. Hood did reach Nashville, but he never captured the place. There was a big battle and he took an awful licking, but I was not there and that is another story. By then, we had left Atlanta for "parts unknown."

Our corps, the 20th or Star Corps, from the white stars on our caps, was formed up then of three divisions and each division had three brigades. The brigades had different numbers of regiments in them.

Before we set out, three days rations were issued to each man. Fifteen days rations for each man were put into our remaining wagons. Each man had to carry, besides his three days rations, never less than forty

Union troops destroying a railroad

rounds of ammunition and his blankets and spare clothes if he had any, but after our previous experience nobody burdened himself with much clothes. It was at this point that we got orders to form regular forage squads. We were told in no uncertain terms that henceforth we must live off the country or go hungry. We did both. We lived off the country and even so, often had nothing to eat for twenty-four hours.

Our marches generally were not severe. By that, I mean the distances we did each day were not so great. But the roads were like lead. It was the beginning of winter and we had rivers and swamps to cross, roads and bridges to build for our artillery and wagons. Our marches averaged about fifteen miles a day. While the distances were nothing, it was the aggravations to the march that were wearying.

There were four army corps on this march; all marching along different roads. Together, they covered a territory about forty miles wide. I don't mean that we were forty miles from one solid wing of the army to the other, but that the foragers and scouts and all covered that much ground. The 15th and 17th Army Corps were called the right wing and the 16th and 20th Corps were called the left wing. The 30th Corps was on the left of all. The right wing was known as the "Army of Tennessee" and was commanded, under General Sherman, by General Oliver O. Howard,* a Methodist lay preacher who had lost one arm in some former battle. The left wing was the

* Editor's note: Major General Oliver O. Howard actually was a West Pointer and career soldier. He was, however, deeply religious. He helped to found a Congregationalist church in

"Army of Georgia," commanded by General Henry Slocum.

Attached to each corps were artillery and cavalry. Then we had two small corps of civil engineers and pontooniers, these last with boats or barges for bridging streams. The separate cavalry force was under General Judson Kilpatrick, known as "Kill Cavalry."

Altogether, Sherman had sixty thousand men. When Hood started off for Nashville with his army, Jeff Davis sent General Joseph Johnston—whom he had relieved a short time before—to confront Sherman. Johnston had forty thousand men, we heard.* Considering we were a long ways from home, with no rear communications, no rations, no reinforcements, while Johnston had all these, it easily gave him the advantage.

A great deal of the country where Sherman made his march was low and swampy and there was much rain. Many swamps and the approaches to rivers had to be corduroyed, by cutting and laying trees and limbs across them until they were as rough and hard as corduroy pants. This had to be done, sometimes for miles, before the wagons could pass. As for the men

---

Washington, D. C.; Howard University (Negro) in Washington, which was named after him, and Lincoln Memorial College at Cumberland Gap, Tennessee, for "poor whites." He lost an arm at the battle of Fair Oaks or Seven Pines, Virginia, in 1862, but continued in the army long afterward.

* Editor's note: Sherman's total force at peak is given in the authoritative *Battles and Leaders of the Civil War*, Volume IV, as 112,819 men, with Johnston's estimated as high as 71,000. Each side suffered casualties of between 30,000 and 40,000, accurate indication of the extreme severity of the fighting in the Atlanta Campaign.

who formed the rear, by the time they reached these places there was no road left for them: just mud, mud, mud, and deep mud, too. Generally the slush ranged from ankle deep to knee deep. There were weeks at a time when our feet were wet all the time.

The advance had a pretty good time compared to those at the rear. In the morning when they set out, the road would not be cut up so badly. The advance always halted for dinner and got into camp early. They had time to bathe their feet, if a stream ran nearby; cut brush to sleep on; put up their dog tents; and, if the foragers had been lucky, cook a fresh supper with something saved for dinner the next day. Those in the center and rear were not likely to have time to cook, even if they had anything to cook.

I wish you could have seen our cooking. Even at best, it was nothing to brag on. Commonly our rations consisted of hard tack, very hard crackers, baked so hard and dry as to resist all actions of the weather and time. These came large and small. Of the small ones, about the size of a soda cracker, we received fifteen for a day's rations. Of the large, about six inches square and less than an inch thick, four made a day's rations. The large ones were as solid as an oak board. They were made in Boston and each cracker was stamped "B.C." We used to declare that that explained their hardness—they were made "Before Christ," as the letters stated.

If we had time, we would soak the hard tack in cold water overnight and fry it in grease for breakfast. Fixed up with pepper and salt, it was not, to our appetites, so bad. With hard tack went "sow belly," or

Building a corduroy road in the woods

fat salt pork, and coffee, sometimes with sugar. Those
were our rations in the field. Our coffee was generally
parched. As we had no coffee mills or grinders, we
would put the parched beans in our tin cups and
pound them with our bayonets, then boil them right
in the cup. Sometimes we would not pound our coffee, but would boil it whole, save the berries, dry
them, then put them neatly in a little sack and trade
the "fresh coffee" to the natives for cornbread, milk,
or butter. Even though once used, the beans still
made very good coffee. Anyhow, it was a fair exchange
for the pies and cakes that we sometimes got in return. No one but a soldier or an ostrich could digest
their pies and cakes.

Sometimes when we foraged a little corn meal or
flour, we would mix it with water, put in a pinch of
salt, and bake it in our frying pans. This made cornbread such as the natives had and went pretty well,
but wheat flour cakes were about as heavy as lead and
just about as digestible. Many times, we did not have
even that. I have stolen the corn from the mules and
horses after it had been put in their boxes, washed
their slobber off of it, and parched and eaten it.

At times we drew what was called desiccated vegetables. This was a composition of everything in the
vegetable world—peas, beans, cabbage, turnips, car-
rots, peppers, onions, beets, radishes, parsnips, pars-
ley—with grass to hold it all together. This mixture
was dried and pressed into pieces an inch square. One
of these pieces, put in water, would swell and swell,
then swell some more, until no one man could eat it
all. We made soup of it. It doesn't sound very palata-

ble, but after a regular diet of hard tack, a change to vegetable soup was not to be despised.

In camp we got, in addition to hard tack rations, some beans and rice, and occasionally a piece of beef instead of pork. If in camp for any length of time, we put up enormous ovens and made a detail act as bakers. We then drew soft bread instead of hard tack, one and one-fourth pounds to a day's ration. But we saw no soft bread on our March to the Sea, except as forage.

While we went through Georgia, except when we were in the swamps, we generally had enough to eat. But when we reached the barren sandhills of the Carolinas, we often went hungry. There just was not any food to be had.

All along the way, in Georgia and the Carolinas, we burned all the railroad tracks and the bridges. It was a sight to behold. A hundred or more men would range along the side of the track, stoop, take hold of the ends of the cross ties, and at the word of command would straighten their backs, bringing up the whole track with them, about breast high. At the next command, they turned it straight up onto the ends of the ties, and at the next, over it would go. The rails would be broken loose from the ties, the ties would be piled on top, and burned. As the middle of the rail became red-hot, two or three men would take each end of the rail, lift it off the fire, and walk in opposite directions around a tree. This really put a twist in the rail. We called this putting an "iron necktie" on the trees. To use the rails again, the Rebs would have both to cut down the trees and reheat and straighten the rails. Miles of track would be done this way.

The Rebs of course would try to prevent this work. They did interrupt us, but we always put out a guard. Besides, one rank would stand by their guns, in readiness for action, while the other rank worked on the rails. This all was done by detachments sent to the right and left of the main column. It was extra work or duty. As we had to regain camp or column before night, we frequently had to make a forced march back. It was said one day that our brigade in going out and back tying "iron neckties," marched sixty miles farther than the column. I know we double-quicked some of the way.*

Louisville, Georgia, we found to be a small place, with no railroad and not many houses then. Two small creeks ran near it. The evening before we reached Louisville, we bummers received orders to be careful as strong enemy forces were near us. A squad of about fifty of us got together and agreed that the easiest way to find provisions was to capture the village. We reasoned that if there were Rebels there, the citizens would not hide their provisions and we knew that once we began the attack all the bummers would join in with us.

Some of us deployed out into the woods at the edge of Louisville and advanced. Every one of us was used to such work and knew just what to do. We found

* Editor's note: One amazing aspect of Strong's combat experiences was the manner in which groups of Federal infantrymen, sometimes of platoon or company strength, would join together informally to wage war without any officers or direction from above. Essentially, it represented a singular manifestation of the American spirit of private enterprise in a war. Here it resulted in the unscheduled capture of a town.

the timber had been cut and felled across the road so as to impede the progress of artillery and cavalry, but we crawled under or climbed over and went ahead. We saw a few Rebels, but they fell back about as fast as we walked, so we had no need to fire and advertise our scheme for getting forage. At that time I picked up a pistol in the road, a little pocket concern, no good to anyone.

The Rebs fell back and went beyond the town. We stopped, loaded up with forage, and then, as we knew the army would soon pass that way we waited for them to come up. Some of the town people, seeing how small our force was, either sent word or signalled to the Rebs. Charging back into town in no time came a lot of Rebel cavalry. But we did not propose to lose our forage. As the Reb cavalry came down upon us, yelling and swearing and swinging their sabers, we got behind houses and barns. They could not know how many of us there were, and more bummers were coming all the time.

Half of us gave them a volley which checked them, then a minute after, the others gave them a volley. That was enough for them. They sailed out of town as fast as they had come. Our first success made us bold, and we stood our ground. Of course, the firing had been heard. Soon foragers came pouring into town on one side and the Rebs came charging back on the other.

We had a stiff little skirmish, but held our forage until the main part of our troops came up. The Rebs then went away and stayed away. The troops went into camp as fast as they arrived near the town. This was quite early in the day, and all of us stayed there until nearly night, when our bugles sounded "Fall in!" and away we went.

I was among a squad that was detailed to burn some cotton here. Our orders were to fire the cotton when the last troops had fallen into line and not before. The sun was just setting as we fired the first building. It was a pretty tight building and packed full of bales of cotton. We fired it and shut the doors. By the time we had the rest of the cotton on fire, we heard an explosion. Looking back at the first building, we saw smoke and flame ascending heavenward and pieces of the burning roof going with it. The building being tight and the doors shut, the gas had no way of escape except to burst the roof off.

We waited until satisfied that the fire could not be extinguished by the citizens. Then we fell in and marched on after the regiment. We marched 'til two in the morning before we went into camp again.

On the march when the boys began to get tired, we would shout, "Music, music!" The band's place in the column was directly behind the colonel. If the colonel felt good-natured, he would order the band to strike up. You can't imagine how much easier it is to march when you have a tune to step by. A tune is played, the drums keeping perfect time. Every so often, the big bass drum beats time. Everybody falls into step, the length and quickness of the step being regulated by the music.

The colonel had his own way of fixing us if we hollered out for music when he didn't want it. The easiest way to carry a gun is slung across your shoulders. About the hardest way when marching, although it makes the prettiest sight, is at right-shoulder arms. Then the entire weight of the gun, right at the lock part, rests in the narrow rut atop your shoulder, a rut that already has knapsack and cartridge-box slings cutting into it.

If the boys kept up their calls for music when the colonel thought we did not need it, he would turn halfway around and back on his horse, tip his hat to one side, and sing out: *"Shoulder Ar—ms!"* Then all the guns would have to go up into the hardest position to carry. The music would strike up, but usually not for long. Pretty soon, the colonel would turn around again and shout, *"Atten-Shun, Regi-Ment!"* Then the music would cease, except for the big drum beating time for us—thump thump thump.

As we entered a town or village, the boys would strike up for themselves and start singing a patriotic song. There were some who were splendid singers, others who could follow a tune, and still others, like myself, who could not sing but would roar out the chorus. We sang such songs as "Rally 'Round the Flag," "We Are Coming, Father Abraham, Three Hundred Thousand Strong," "We'll Hang Jeff Davis on a Sour Apple Tree," "Tramp, Tramp, Tramp, the Boys are Marching," "Just Before the Battle, Mother," and "Old Brother Wise Stuck His Goggles on His Eyes."*

If we remained in the town any time, we always

* Editor's note: "Rally 'Round the Flag" was, of course, "The Battle Hymn of the Republic." "We'll Hang Jeff Davis on a Sour Apple Tree" was the identical tune, originally a Southern camp meeting song to which Southerners set the words, "We'll Hang John Brown on a Sour Apple Tree" in 1859–60. The song about "Old Brother Wise" was a comic tune making fun of the wartime Governor of Virginia.

found a house where there were singers. As soon as
the girls would recover from their fright at the sight
of us, they and our singers would take turns-about
singing. They sang their patriotic airs, and our boys
the Union ones.

At one fine house, there was a piano. One of our
boys asked permission to play it. The oldest girl replied, "I can't stop you. You can get on it and play it
with your feet if you want to." So he sat down and
played tunes that were common everywhere, such as
"Home Sweet Home." Then he asked the girls to join
in singing, and they did. So did a lot of the boys.
Everyone had a fine time and became good-natured.
When the oldest girl was asked to play for us, she said
she would if she could play her own selection. Of
course, we agreed. She played and sang "Dixie." We
cheered and called for more. That pleased them, and
she and others played and sang "The Bonnie Blue
Flag." Then our men sang "Yankee Doodle Dandy"
and "Hail Columbia."

As we left the house, the boys sang "The Girl I
Left Behind Me." We were all so pleased that we took
almost nothing from them, in fact, advised them how
to hide provisions so that other foragers would not
find them. So much for the powers of song and
courtesy.

Courtesy, as usual, worked both ways. We met it
with an old gentleman at Madison, Georgia. A few
days after leaving Atlanta, we came to the town of
Madison, one of the finest and neatest villages that we
passed through. It was surrounded by a rich, level
country. The houses were mansions, with large hand-

some grounds, and the nigger huts were all neatly whitewashed. The town was laid off in wide, clean streets, each side of the street lined with rows of magnolias, live oaks, and mulberry trees.

The houses at Madison were mostly of brick, surrounded by wide porches. Each house had from one to three halls running through it. The second stories also had halls and porches, the latter covered up the sides with climbing roses, honeysuckle, and other such runners. The gardens were ornamented with bronze statuary in the likeness of lions and other animals. Each mansion had a long driveway leading from the road, lined with magnolias or live oaks. It was all a perfect paradise.

So far as I know, no property of any kind was destroyed here. The old gentlemen who were at home, while strong Rebels, were gentlemen. The ladies were ladies, neatly dressed, and the children were well behaved. The people were very hospitable, even to us their enemies. They were smart about it, too.

The day we passed through Madison, our regiment had the extreme rear, with our company out behind to prevent straggling. I, with four men, had the corporal's guard at the very end of all. We made our last halt a mile outside of town, in front of a splendid house. Soon we were surrounded by children, black and white, some of them lying on the grass.

When we halted, an old gentleman at the house arose, saluted us, and asked if we were thirsty. He ordered a number of niggers to serve us with water. He said he was sorry that water was all he had to offer us, but the army had stripped him of everything else. He had been feeding them all day as they passed, he said, and had his servants bring them cooked food until his larder was empty. We could believe him, for the evidence lay all over the road—bones picked clean, empty cotton baskets that had been full of bread. His grounds looked so clean and untrodden that I asked him if he had been molested in any way.

"No," he said. "I made up my mind when I found your people were coming this way that I would keep my temper and be civil, and feed them as far as I could. I have done so and I have not been disturbed. I have nothing to complain of, but I am very tired, as I have sat here since daylight. Your people have been passing for all day long."

At that the old lady added, "I never saw so many men. More people have passed here today than I supposed there were in the world. Surely, you must be the last?"

One of our boys, a kind of smart-aleck, up and said, "Oh, no, Ma'am, we are just the advance of Hooker's corps. It will be four days before Hooker's corps will all get by here, and there are four more corps just as large on other roads."

"My God, we might just as well give up now!" the old lady exclaimed and threw up her hands.

When you remember that we actually were the last of Hooker's corps, and that they had been passing ever since daylight, you won't wonder at the old lady's despair at the lie Dick told her. But the old gent's shrewdness in feeding such a multitude saved him much annoyance.

While nobody harmed the old gent's farm, he did,

come to think of it, lose what he no doubted regarded as part of his property. All through this section, the niggers were nearly always a happy, careless set, many of them loving their Mass'r and Missus above their own children and being proud to belong to such a fine family. Many, however, were dissatisfied with their lot. Numbers flocked to us and refused to return to their masters, although we told them we had no way to feed them or care for them.

While we were there at the mansion at Madison, the niggers asked us if it was true that they were free. We told them they would be free if the North gained the war, which we were sure to do as the war was about over. Pretty soon, an old darky and his wife came to us, each with a bundle on their heads. The old gent says, "Where are you and Dinah going?" The old darky replied: "We is free, Massa, and while we love you, Massa, and Missus and the children, we is going to go 'long with these Yankees." We quickly told them they were foolish and had better stay where they were until the close of the war. We told them they did not know what they would have to endure with us; that we never knew where we would sleep or where our next meal could be found; that we were daily in danger of having a fight; and that if we got into a fight and got whipped, you darkies will surely be killed by the Rebs. "Can't help it, young Massa," the old darky says. "We's going on with you. We can do as much as you can. We will cook and wash for you, and let you rest."

The old gent broke in, "Daniel, h'ain't I been a good master to you and let you . . ."

"Yes, Massa."

"Did I ever whip you or Dinah?"

"No, Massa."

"Then stay with me. You and I were boys together. Don't leave me now."

The two darkies cried as only niggers can cry, but the old man said, "We must go, freedom is as sweet to us as it is to you. God bless Massa Henry, and Missy, and the young massas and misses, but we's going." And go with us they did.

We took along the old nig and his wife to cook for our mess. We told them if they would cook for us, we would divide with them, and cautioned them that if they saw a smokehouse, they were to hunt for hams or bacon. That night I got the big mess kettle, filled it up and got the water boiling, and stripped off my lousy clothes and had the nigs wash and boil and dry them by the fire while I sat wrapped in a blanket. While they stayed with us, they did our cooking. When we had night marches, the nigs would go ahead and catch a pig or chickens, build a fire, and by the time we came up would have a hot meal ready for us. We would take some chicken in one hand and a roast potato in the other, and eat as we marched. Old Dinah proved to be a modest woman, and very motherly. She would talk for hours about old Massa and Missy, or the children that she had nursed for the Missus, and then she would cry and cry. Homesick, I guess. She and her husband stayed with us for two weeks, then went to cook for some officer.

Meantime, as we went along, thousands and thousands of niggers flocked to us. They would come on foot, on mules or on horses stolen from their masters.

Sometimes they would steal the family carriage and team, load it up with everything at hand, and come to us that way. Many times the women and girls would dress up in their mistress' clothes. Sometimes if they had on an old ragged dress, they would have her fine hat or bonnet on their head. Often the men would wear the master's plug hat or a pair of his gloves, and not much else.

Of course this swarm of niggers was not allowed to march with us, as they would obstruct the road. They had to take to the fields or fall in behind the column. On the march or in camp, they were a happy, ignorant set, knowing no care nor responsibility. They took no thought for the morrow. Like pigs, if their bellies were full they were happy. At night after a hard day's march, they would sing and dance long after all the soldiers but the guards were asleep. If they were hungry, they would beg of anyone. The women were not noted for their modesty or virtue, and who can wonder at it. Some of the women were so indifferent about such things that when they came to a creek or swamp, they would elevate their clothes if necessary to the tops of their heads, and so wade through.

What became of these swarms of niggers, I do not know. Some of the men entered the service, and regiments of United States Colored Troops were formed out of them. At Savannah, Georgia, and later at Goldsborough, North Carolina, they organized guard camps and had rations issued to them.

Despite a spate of skirmishes between foragers and southern cavalry or militia, not one major battle occurred between Atlanta and Savannah. There were minor struggles to seize and wreck railroads, and to defend Union wagon trains from Confederate raids—nothing more. The rest was march, march, march, sometimes on empty stomachs when the foragers failed to produce food.

a private cease-fire along the chattahoochee

AFTER OUR first day's march out from Atlanta toward Savannah, I had been on the skirmish line all day. We and the enemy's skirmishers spent the whole day shooting at each other. A small river separated us, with a long, low sandbar about in the middle of the river.

Just about sundown, a Reb sings out, "Say, Yanks, I want to talk to you a minute. If you won't shoot, I'll get out on top of our rail pile" (their pickets piled up rails, the same as ours did, to sit and lean on and also to get behind while shooting).

We called back that we would not shoot without warning, "Unless you begin first." So the word passed down, along both sides of the river, for both Rebs and Yanks to cease firing because "the boys are going to gas a little."

Someone asked the Rebs if they had any tobacco to trade. "Yes," came the reply. "Have you'uns got any coffee?" Back we came, "Yes, meet us out on that sandbar without arms and bring some newspapers." So a number of us from each side laid down our arms, stripped off our clothes, and swam and waded out to the sandbar.

There, squatting around naked as two tribes of savages, we made our exchange, coffee for tobacco. We told each other stories of the war, what we had seen of it, shook hands, and went back each to our own sides. Then we dressed ourselves, picked up our arms, asked the Rebs if they were dressed.

"Yes," came back the call from across the river. "Hunt your holes, we are going to shoot!" So we began again to do our best to kill each other.

This kind of little, local peace in the midst of bloodshed soon became a common occurrence, mostly in places where there was a river or some other natural separation line that pinned down skirmishers awhile.

When we lay along the Chattahoochee River in Georgia, the Rebs and we agreed not to fire at each other except by order of an officer. If such orders were given either of us, we were to notify the other side before we began firing. We told each other across the river, which was about twenty to thirty rods wide, that the war was all nonsense and that if we did kill a man once in a while, it would have no effect on the war as a whole. So we agreed not to do it except under special orders.

I don't remember as our officers at this time ever told us to begin firing. But occasionally as the Yanks on our side of the river and the Rebs on their side were taking it easy—some resting atop of our rail piles, some asleep—the Rebs would sing out, "Look out, Yanks, we are going to shoot!"

Then a change came over the quiet scene. Bedlam broke loose. If a man showed as much as an arm or a leg, it was instantly made a target. Woe to the man who showed enough of himself to hold a bullet! This would last perhaps an hour. Then someone on one side or the other would shout, "Hold on, Yank," or "Johnnie," as the case might be, "Let's stop this."

It soon came to be understood by us that they, the Rebs, were ordered to do about so much firing every so often, but they always gave us notice—except once when they barely managed. That one evening, just before sundown, as we were taking it easy on both sides, a Rebel officer came galloping up on his horse. He jumped down and began cursing and swearing at his men for not shooting the d——d Yanks.

"Talking with them, are you?" he roared. "Well, begin firing and shoot h——l out of them!" We could hear everything he said, and took up our guns. They yelled to us to "hunt our holes."

Little Charlie Hapgood of our regiment, a splendid shot, says "I'll *fix* him." We all stood watching as Charlie fired. The Rebel officer threw up his arms over his head, staggered a step or two, and fell dead. Then we cheered and cheered, and called out across the river, "Say, Johnnie, is it time to hunt our holes yet?" They said, "No, he was a damn fool, anyway, and deserved what he got." So everything settled down again and we had no more firing.

Sometimes it got grim. At one place our lines got so close that we could toss hand grenades* into each other's breastworks. No man on either side dared to show his head even a second, but all fired from under headlogs.

At one time, just after the battle in which the Rebs had charged our line and lost heavily, we got to talking back and forth, the breastworks were so close together. As each army tried to hide its numbers, we did not expect a truthful answer to one question that we asked them but we asked it anyhow. "How many men has Johnston got?" One big, strapping Reb said, "Oh, about enough for another killin'."

In one fight during the Atlanta campaign, our regiment was on the extreme left and our company was away out ahead on the skirmish line. We were advancing, firing, advancing again, to drive the enemy's skirmishers in. There was so much noise that the commands could not always be distinctly heard. At one command, "By the left flank!" our company did not hear it and kept advancing toward the enemy. We supposed, of course, that our support was right

---

* Editor's note: Several types of fragmentation hand grenades, set off on contact by percussion caps, were used in the Civil War when lines became static and entrenchments grew strong. In rifle pits, the "headlog" was a solid log or tree laid horizontally, with its ends imbedded in earth and an opening underneath to form a slot or loophole in the front of the trench. The log protected the shooter's head, hence the term.

behind us, whereas it had turned away at an angle and the gap between us widened with every step.

We came to a narrow but deep creek, with no good cover on our side. So we plunged into the creek. It came up to our waists, and we had to hold our haversacks and cartridge boxes up high to keep them dry. There was a huge fallen tree on the other bank of the creek. Just after we crossed and got near to the tree, twenty-five or thirty men ran out from behind it and jumped into some timber below. It was so sudden we did not get a good look at their uniforms, and, besides, all uniforms had begun to look alike what with the rain and sun always working on them.

We could not believe that we were so near to the Rebs that part of them were in our line, but I was sure they were Rebs. Rickert, next to me, was sure they were Yanks. We got down along the other side of the tree while they fell back behind other trees.

"What troops are you?" I calls. "Have you got behind?" Rickert, by me, says, "Yes, we are all right."

From up in the trees, an officer says, "What regiment are you?"

"One Hundred and Fifth Illinois", says I. "Who are you?"

"Come up into the line," orders the officer.

Rickert still thought them Yanks and wanted to move up in line with them. I said no.

This officer still continued our talk, with his men hid behind trees and ours behind the big log. All but me, I was excited and forgot to hide.

When the officer found he could not coax us up

into his line, he stepped out and says to his men, "Give them hell, kill them!"

All in one breath, he called to me, "Come out here or I'll kill you!"

While his men stepped out from behind the trees and began shooting, our men jumped up and returned the fire. The officer came right at me. He was not more than twenty rods away when he ordered me to surrender and leveled his revolver at me.

My gun was resting in my hand, uncocked, with the butt on the ground. At such times, one thinks and acts quickly. I knew I had no time to waste, so I brought my right foot up, pushed down with my foot until I heard the hammer snap as it raised into full-cock position, then brought my gun up and fired, all while you could draw a breath.

The Rebel colonel—for he was a colonel—threw up his arms and over he went. But not before firing at me. His ball hit the log just in front of me and brushed my clothes. From the time he ordered his men to fire at us, and he and I fired at each other, was not more than ten seconds. It was all done in a breath, and we had the Rebs on the run.

We decided we had got too far ahead of our men, so we pushed into the creek again and went back to our lines, this time expecting to be shot by mistake for Rebels.

Later in the day, with support, we went across the creek and over the same ground again. We came across a number of dead Rebs, among them this colonel. One of us took a letter out of his pocket. It was to his wife and said that they would "soon have the Yankee scum killed off and then I'll be home." The poor fellow never got there. He ought to have run if he wanted to see his wife again, but I reckon his time had come.

That night around our camp fire, we told of our day's adventures and then shook one another by the hand. We found that in this fight we had one man captured by the enemy, Joe Hammersmith.

Next I must tell you of what I remember as a sort of manhunt. Again, we were away out in advance, but were marching along easily, not expecting there was an enemy near us.

First came a corporal and four men, me amongst them. Then a sergeant and eight men. Then a little behind them came the company and then the regiment.

Each man at this point was expected to have his gun loaded. But as we were also expected to have our guns clean inside and out, and loading dirtied them, most of our guns were unloaded.

We in the advance five were swinging along as gay as you please. We had just reached the far edge of a woods. The road led out through a lane with fields on each side, and beyond the fields were more woods.

"Ping!" came a bullet by us. By this time, we knew the song of a bullet as well as we did each others' voices. Without any order, as I well remember, our guns came butt to the ground, we each bit off the end of a cartridge, and loaded and capped the guns, then began to look for the enemy.

By now, bullets were whistling among us and one

man had been shot through the hand. Well, we knew our work. We knew that we four unwounded ones had to cross that field, if we could, and find what was in the woods beyond. So we deployed out, keeping a lookout ahead, but could see nothing but puffs of smoke.

The eight men behind came up, deployed out with us, and away with a rush we went across the field. Still all we could see was puffs of smoke and all we could hear was "pings" of bullets. We wasn't long crossing that field. As we drew near the far side, the enemy pulled back into the woods. They kept firing at us as we came on. Once in a while, we would see a man dodge from one tree to another, and would shoot at him.

We drove them pretty briskly, and concluded that they only wanted to delay us and not bring on a general fight. Out through the woods we went and into another field. On the far side of this field, the Rebs had put together a number of piles of rails as protection from our shots. It looked bad for us to have to cross this narrow field in the face of protected riflemen, but we were hunting these men and had to drive them out. So we made a rush straight across the field, not stopping to fire although we received their fire. They did not wait for us, but left for the next woods. Then it was our turn to shoot. So we gave them our volley and chased them again, loading as we ran. They hid behind trees and again checked our rush. We kept firing as we went ahead. Every little while a Reb would shoot and then run for a tree farther away.

But one fellow would not run. He loaded and fired,

Skirmishing in the woods

but kept to his tree until we were close to him, within a few feet. Then he took his gun in his left hand. As he went back, he looked over his shoulder at us and slapped his backside at us in derision, and said some pretty bad words. Some one of us shouted, "Shoot him, shoot him, kill him, the Rebel s—— of a b——!" Others shouted, "No, don't kill him, let him go. It would be a pity to kill so brave a man." So no one shot at him. We yelled at him and cheered him as he ran, and in a minute more we began our advance again.

This time they did not stop at all. They ran through a swamp and here I picked up a silver-mounted revolver that one of them must have dropped. I had no use for it and gave it to someone else.

We followed them to the edge of another field. About sixty rods away from us was a lane leading up to a house. In the lane were the Rebs. Their horses had been held there waiting for them, and they had now reached the horses. Rebs and horses were all in a huddle, each man trying to mount and get away.

On the porch of the house was an old man, and four or five women. There was a moment of confusion among us, though not over the people on the porch. Scott, our company commander, was now up with us. He and some others thought for a moment, upon seeing the horses, that a detachment of our own cavalry had intercepted the Rebs. This idea lasted but a moment. Then Scott says, "Every man rest his gun on the fence or against a tree, and fire a volley on command." When we were all ready, most of the Rebs

were mounted. We gave a shout and poured our fire
into them.

What a scattering there was! The women on the
porch ran into the house, screaming and crying. The
Rebs laid down on their horses as flat as they could,
and pounded the horses' sides with their heels to get
going. The horses snorted and reared up, some dashing off without any rider. The dismounted men ran
into the nearby orchard and the skirmish was over.

In the house we found several wounded men.
When I and others went in, the women had not yet
gotten over their scare. Their faces were as white as
flour.

Shortly, we resumed our march. We had many such
scrapes as this, but I particularly remember this one
because of the man who refused so long to run, because of the easy shot that we got at the Rebs in the
lane, and because of the scared women.

To make marching easier, it was ordered that the
troops that had the lead today should take the rear
tomorrow. The center today would be the advance
tomorrow, and the rear today would be the center tomorrow. Thus all took turns at the lead, which was
the easiest place for marching, if not fighting, and at
the rear, which was the hardest.

The advance would always leave camp about daybreak. As soon as they moved off in column, the center would follow, then the rear.

The wagons were always in the center to prevent
their being captured. Behind each wagon would be a
soldier to act as guard, and behind so-many wagons a
company or perhaps a regiment. In this manner, the

center would be sandwiched, wagons and soldiers. Each wagon had six mules and a driver. The driver, sometimes a white soldier and sometimes a nigger contraband, would have a saddle on lefthand wheel or hind mule, with a small rope leading to the head mule's bridle. He always rode and always drove the six mules with one line or rope. Over his shoulder he carried a long, heavy whip. He would "touch up" any mule in his train with the lash when necessary.

The wagons had no brakes, because the drivers could not use them, not being on a seat or in position to put on brakes. Unless the road was too steep, the wheel mules would hold the wagon back in going downhill. If the hill was too steep, the driver would dismount and lock the wheels of his wagon. At the bottom, he would dismount again and unlock them. This took time, and when every teamster in the line would do this, you can easily see what a delay it caused.

It rained more or less all the time, and so many feet, so many horses and mules, so many wagons, soon cut up the road so bad that an old-fashioned Illinois road would have been in comparison like a turnpike. The soldiers would have to "pay out" the wagons, lifting at the wheels. The teamsters would swing their big whips at the mules and cuss, and the wagons would get stuck again.

When the going got too bad, we had to build a corduroy road for the wagons. We would tear down rail fences and carry the rails to the mudhole and throw them in until the solid road was ready. After a few more wagons had passed, the road would get bad

again and more rails would have to be used. When
the rails gave out, we would use saplings.

The Rebels were as much bother as their mud.
Even in small numbers, they would do all they could
to annoy us. They would often make a dash at our
wagon train and attempt to kill the mules, drivers and
guards when they could. This they could do, as each
wagon had only the one guard on it, and squads of
fifty to one hundred guards distributed at intervals
along the train.

The country being heavily timbered, and the
Rebels knowing every by-road and bridle path, it was
no hard matter for them to dash out of some by-road,
scatter the drivers, and if they could stampede the
guards, then shoot the mules. This of course would
cause some of the wagons to be abandoned for lack
of mules.

However, the Rebs seldom succeeded in driving
away the guards. As their object was not to fight, but
to destroy the wagon train in a small-scale operation,
they seldom did much damage. Their numbers usually were quite small. But as the drivers were generally niggers or hired citizens, who were hired only
to drive, not fight like soldiers, they usually ran and
left the guards to defend the teams and wagons.

At such times, it was comical to see the drivers
jump off their mules and rush into the woods. Sometimes they would jump from one mule to another,
on the other side, and in their haste fall down and
roll over and over, shouting all the time for the
guards to "look out dar, de Rebs is a-coming!"

When on guard duty, we usually put our guns in

the feed box on the back of the wagons so as not to have to carry them. I was train guard one day, and put my blankets, haversack and gun in the feed box. I carried only my cartridge box and canteen of water, for water was precious on hot days.

Suddenly I heard the nigger driver yell out, "Gawd Amighty, dar dey come!" Of course, I knew who "dey" was but I was half asleep as I tramped along behind the wagon. I grabbed my gun and jumped to the right side of the wagon.

All the way down the train to the front, the drivers were leaping from their mules. They always rode the lefthand rear mule and as "dey" were coming from the left, the drivers were climbing over the off mules to get away. Even in my hurry to get a sight and a shot at the Rebs, the picture was painted on my brain and I can see it yet: the niggers piling over the mules, some alighting on their heels, some on their heads, some on all fours running like dogs. Some ran for the timber and would tumble into the underbrush with a whoop. All this did not take a quarter of a minute.

I walked to the left side of my wagon and there the Rebs were, coming on horseback. Just as I stepped out from behind the wagon, a Reb rode up, revolver in hand. He halted and brought his pistol up to shoot. It took him so long to "take aim" that I had time to finish him if I had wanted to. I suppose he thought all the guards had run away, for he talked like this to himself:

"A d——n fine train of wagons. I wish I could send them home, but as I can't I'll fix them."

My first thought was to kill him, and if he had

begun firing I probably would have. Instead, I says "Surrender!" He started in his saddle, looked at me, made a motion to bring his pistol to bear on me. I shot him through the leg, breaking his leg and killing his horse.

I then turned to get behind the wagon and reload, before the next Reb to come along picked me off. That Reb went on the run for the woods, as fast as his horse could take him. So did the rest. They killed a few mules before running, but not enough to delay the train.

As soon as the shooting faded out, my driver came back. We picked up the Reb whose leg I broke, as a prisoner, and put him into a wagon with a few more that had been captured. Then we went on. Probably we had not been delayed five minutes by the whole business. It was a fair sample of the everyday duties of a train guard.

A short quick dash from the woods or some cross-road by a few rebel cavalry, perhaps several mules killed, maybe a guard killed or wounded, maybe a Reb killed or captured, maybe no damage on either side—that was it. The Rebels always had to work quick and fast at this business, for as soon as any firing was heard, the strong squad of which I spoke hurried up and reinforced the individual guards. Two to five minutes was as long as such squabbles lasted, but they were exciting while they lasted.

For spells this train guard duty could go on and on. The advance always broke camp at daylight and if the center with the wagons had not come up in time for us soldiers to take the advance, those who had it the

Confederates attack a wagon train

day before would have it again that day. Many a time have I been obliged to march all night, get into camp at last, and, having had no sleep, be obliged to pull out again and keep going. Sometime we would not even have time to boil coffee, but would take a hard-tack and a piece of raw pork meat and eat it on the march. When our crackers gave out, which they did in a few days, we were lucky to have anything to eat. What we foraged was, of course, uncooked. Our foragers would, when they got back to our lines of march, cook the stuff for the boys and have it ready when they came up. But often the foragers would not find anything. Then, if we had nothing left over, we went hungry.

Of one thing the wagons had a supply, and that was coffee. Each boy had a tin cup. If we halted for any purpose anywhere near noon, multitudes of fires would be started and each boy would make a cup of coffee. No one who has not been tired and hungry can know how good a cup of coffee tastes and how much it can and does liven up a person.

The advance nearly always got into camp, at the place the officers picked, by three o'clock and sometimes by two, and had plenty of time to rest. If the center and rear only came up in time to rest that night, and take their proper places in turn as before described, then everything was all right.

Halting for the wagons to be pulled out of the mud, however, made us have many night marches. The season was getting cool and as we would halt, we would burn what fence rails had not been used to build roads. For miles and miles, there would be a line of fires on each side of the road. As night would come on, the boys would begin to start fires.

When we were marching in the extreme rear in our turn, we would see their fires ahead and say, "Well, there is camp, only a little further to go, boys." Then when we got to the place, it would be only a roadside fire of rails. So we would add a rail, warm a minute, and guess the next fire we could see ahead would be camp. Only to be fooled again and again.

In case the fences were all burned we never disturbed an occupied house. If only there was furniture left in a house, we never disturbed it. The only houses we took to make fires of were *empty houses,* reckoning the owners of such houses to be *rank Rebels.*

That the Confederates would surrender Savannah, an important seaport, without a tremendous battle was beyond the Union army's fondest dreams. Sure enough, they marched up against the most formidable fortifications and heaviest guns they had encountered. To find a "back door" to Savannah, they bridged swamps. Then a key fort fell. . . .

 # "our bullets will make sieves of your hides..."

ONE DAY as we were marching along a wide, macadamized road, we suddenly heard the booming of cannon. By the deep sound, we knew that they were none of the guns we had brought with us. At the time, we were near the Savannah River but nowhere near the sea, as the river runs far inland. Yet we quickly recognized the heavy, sullen roar as the big ship guns of the navy. Compared with them, the smaller guns that we had with us would have sounded like popguns beside shotguns. From the distance of the sound, we knew that the fight was far off and not for us. As it turned out, Savannah was still seventy miles away. Our fleet must have been many miles closer to the city than we were at the moment, working up the river toward it while we marched down.

Instantly, the air was full of guesses as to what was going on. What if Admiral Porter had entered the channel and was bombarding the city? Would the navy capture the place before we got there? You can imagine how anxious we were to know, but we could not as we had no means of communication.

The sound, though, was inspiring. Somewhere ahead of us there were Yankees and we were bound to find them. As we knew by this time that Savannah was our destination, we marched on with light hearts, for the firing could be nowhere except at or below Savannah, between that river port and the sea.

When we reached there and opened communications with the fleet, there would be bread and meat and news, and best of all, letters from home for us. Not much was said of home, the minds of every man and boy were full of the thoughts of it.

Well, the road was good, and there was no mud to stall the wagon mules. We marched along at the rate of four miles an hour by the mileposts. I remember how gleefully we counted the mileposts—70-69-68-67—and every one nearer to rest and letters and word from home. All of us, officers and privates, were excited. The "boom, boom" of the cannon seemed to put new spirits and "jump" into our legs.

We found a high, broad and almost straight road to the city. On either side, as we traveled, were cotton fields, or rice plantations knee-deep with water. One day we saw troops filing off into the woods on our right. As we came up, we passed their camp. They were in a place not long ago held by the Rebs. We had a plain view of it. Not a hundred rods in front of us were strong entrenchments, with cannon that had mouths big enough to crawl into. We had reached almost to Savannah, but we *did not* have the city.

Before we finally got to the city, we had plenty of good hard work but next to no fighting; many adventures and some escapes which, if I don't forget, I'll tell you of.

That night we went into camp just to the right of the road we had been traveling, between it and the main railroad track. In front of us was an irrigating canal used years ago for a rice plantation, but it had been abandoned by order of the authorities because the stagnant water made the city unhealthy. This canal was six or eight rods wide, but the banks had caved in, making it much wider.

Now the sad thing for us about this canal was that we soon had to build a bridge across it. Not only had the railroad track been torn up but the railroad bridge across the canal had been burned. The only remaining approach to the city was down the turnpike we had traveled, but guarding that bridge were strong breastworks defended by heavy cannon and infantry. The road wound back and forth through their entrenchments in something like an M shape, and anyone who tried to travel it was sure to face plenty of fire from all directions. The entrenchments were six feet high, with ditches six feet deep in front and some filled with water from the Savannah River. Where there was no water, the distance from the bottom of the ditch to top of entrenchments was about twelve feet.

In front of the works, pointing toward us, were

from two to four rows of what we used to jokingly call "hayracks," only they were no joke. They consisted of large logs with holes bored through them and sharpened stakes put through the holes close together. We had met these before, and had to stop and remove them, with the Rebs firing at us all the while. It was no very pleasant or safe piece of work.

Well, we looked over all this, and expected we would have to charge these strong works. As it turned out, however, we did not have to do so, for which we were thankful.

For two days, we did nothing much but picket duty and foraging. The foraging didn't amount to much except for rice. For ten days, rice boiled without salt was all we had to eat. We even roasted the rice and made coffee of it. I got so much rice during that time that I seldom eat it now. Other troops fared even worse than we did. Everybody went hungry, but everybody was good-natured because we felt sure we would capture the city soon. We thought that when we captured it, we would either hold it and make excursions against the Rebs from it, or be sent north by water. We couldn't imagine any more long marches. Little did anyone but Sherman and Grant know!

In two days, we were ordered to make a little advance to straighten out our lines. Our regiment only advanced a few rods. We could not go farther without getting into a swamp. The enemy probably thought we needed scaring, for they lit into us with their big guns. These threw a shell bigger than a water pail and the shells came shrieking down among us. However, I don't remember that a single one burst among us. All went beyond us. At first, the racket of the big guns and the horrible shrieks of their huge shells startled the best of us. We were used to cannon, but not such bellowing fellows as these. It did not take us long, though, to find out that they didn't hurt us.

Every morning just at sunrise, the Rebs would give us a few noisy rounds. They had the range pretty well, so for half an hour every morning we lay very close to the ground behind the works we had built. The Rebels used not only these very big guns but smaller ones and the infantry added their fire, too.

We soon found out that we of the army had no cannon with us big enough to knock their breastworks to pieces or to silence their guns. So it looked like we had to be there until the river below the city should be opened. Some of the troops were sent to help the navy capture the fort between the city and the ocean. Any history will tell you how it was done.

Meantime we had work to do. The breastworks across the canal on the road were the only ones in position to see our troops and annoy them. To try to silence those guns, and also to keep the boys in practice, we were ordered to build rifle pits on our end of the road as near to their line as possible. This of course had to be done when ordered.

One night the orderly sergeant came along, paper in hand, and called off the names of the boys who were detailed for this work. It took me. We were instructed to leave everything in camp but our guns, ammunition, and canteens. We took pickaxes and spades, and just at dark reported at headquarters. The boys who gathered looked pretty solemn. We knew at that point that something desperate was to be done, but had not been told what. Then we were told. We were to go as near the Reb guns as we could, and dig rifle pits for sharpshooters to lie in during the day and snipe at the gunners.

"Now boys," said the officer in charge, "this is nasty work but it must be done. As soon as the Johnnies find out we are here, they will begin to throw *store kettles* at us." (We knew he meant big shells.) "I don't want one of you to open your mouth. Obey everything I order instantly. I will watch their breastworks, and when I see a flame, I'll sing out 'Lie down!' and then you drop."

It was a dark, raining night. We fixed our traps so they would not rattle, and went out into the road. Within forty or fifty rods of their works, we lay down. With our shovels we scratched a hole in the road and put the dirt in front of us. In an hour, we had a hole across the road maybe a foot deep. But we could do no more without using our picks and that would be sure to arouse the Rebs.

The captain in charge says in a whisper, "All ready? Now use your picks quick and fast, and for God's sake drop when I say NOW." So we rose to our feet and worked as if our lives depended on it. I suppose the Rebel guards did not know at first what the noise was. Anyway, we made our hole quite a bit bigger and deeper, throwing the dirt toward the Rebs. Then the cap sang out "NOW!" and down we went.

It seems as if I was not halfway down when the heavens lit up, big shells shrieked over us, and then came a roar, all in a second. The big guns roared and banged and cracked away at us for half an hour, then stopped. Captain says, "Get to work." We did. In a few minutes, captain sings, "Down!" And so it was, down and up and down, all night long.

Just before daybreak, a sharpshooter from the 102nd Illinois and his partner came up, took possession of the rifle pits, and remained there all day in plain sight of the Rebs and not more than fifty rods from them. The sharpshooter kept peppering away at whatever moved. The Rebs dared not charge these rifle pits, as our guns and boys in the rear of the pits had just as much of a chance to shoot down that road as the Rebs did.

Joe, the sharpshooter, stuck it out all alone as we later found out. Joe told me that just after sunrise, his comrade showed too much of his head and was killed by a Rebel bullet. Joe remained on the job until night, with his dead friend beside him. He said he killed thirty-three Rebs that day. That night, a strong force was sent to relieve him and to keep the Rebs from sending out a party to capture the pit. The next day, more sharpshooters went out, and so it went on.

Next we went to work to bridge the place where the railroad bridge across the canal or swamp had been burnt out. At the same time that one party was sent to dig the rifle pit, another was given axes and ordered to cut down live oak trees as near to the canal as they could be found. Soon I was busy with that. We cut them in lengths of eight to ten feet in the daytime, and brought them close to the canal. At night, the boys took them and sunk them loghouse fashion in the water, to serve as piers or uprights for a bridge we were to build across the canal later right in the face of the enemy. Live oaks will not float. So we placed the bottom ones, then one man swam into the water each time and held them in place while others of us piled more on top. Other piles were sunk and laid farther out. Log stringers were placed on them, and held down by long poles which were pinned to the stringers.

The Rebs knew what we were doing almost as soon as we began. Then we had to go back a piece to cut the big logs. At night when their sharpshooters could not see us, we would bring up the logs by hand to the bank and lay the bridge.

Many funny things happened and were said at that point. The Rebel pickets came right down to the edge of the swamp not twenty rods from us and sometimes fired at us, sometimes talked at us. They cracked many a joke. They asked why we were building the bridge, when the easiest way to get into the city would be to walk right in along the road and surrender. They asked if we expected them to keep still and let us finish the bridge. They shouted, "As soon as you get close enough for us to see you, our bullets will make sieves of your hides."

One thing that kept down the murder at this point was the denseness of everything in the swamp. I should have mentioned before now that the cypress trees and tropical vines grew so thick that we had to cut every step of our way with axes.

We joked back at the Rebs by asking them to begin on their side and build out to meet us. We offered them rice if they would. We also asked them the news. They responded that Lee had captured Grant and was on his way to whip Sherman. We knew better than that, of course, and asked them to give us something fresh.

Farther back in Georgia, we had picked up a local Union man. In asking what troops were in front of us, this man found a Georgia regiment that had been raised near his home. So he asked if so-and-so, by name, was there. "Yes, who are you?" came back. Our men told his name, and a good many Rebs inquired that way about "my wife," or "my folks." Our man answered all, according to what he knew about them. This made quite a session. When they were relieved, they would sing across, "Goodbye, Jim," or "John," or whoever.

While at work on the bridge, the Rebs often shelled us and fired at us with musketry. One time when we were sinking a lot of live oak logs into place, we had one pier built up above the water. A number of us were standing on it to hold the logs in place, also to place other logs as stringers. The Rebs began shelling us. It was dark as the inside of a coat pocket. As they could not see us, they aimed at our noise. One of our men would always watch for the flash of their guns and warn us to lie down, but we on the logs had no place to lie down.

Along came a shell, hit our pile of logs, and knocked them forty ways or more. We who were standing on the logs took a tumble into the water. It was winter and the water was cold. We went down with the logs, first a log on top, then a man, then a log. Some hollered for help. The boys on the shore shouted for fun.

The Rebs could hear our uproar and they shouted over to ask what was the matter. We told them they had knocked the underpinning from our bridge and had us all swimming. They replied that they could do it every time, but would not, as they were anxious for us to finish the bridge—so we could cross it and surrender. We told them we were anxious to get across, too, and if they would stay there until the bridge was finished, we would come put rings in their noses and make show animals of them.

Our bridge went slow but we were getting on with it. In the meantime, we could hear heavy cannonading every day down on the coast. We were anxious to open communications with the fleet as we were very tired of our rice diet. Rumors were our steadiest diet. One rumor would have it that Fort McAllister, on the nearby Ogeechee River, had fallen; next, that the fort had not been captured, then some other contradictory report. Fort McAllister was supposed to be the "key" to Savannah.

Our clothes were worn out, our shoes were full of holes, and many had no shoes at all—nothing but gunny sacks tied around their feet. Our regiment could have appeared with success as ragamuffins in a play or political campaign. We had no soap, and the dirt and grime and soot and grease and smoke from burning so many pine knots on our march would not come off without soap and hot water. We were as brown as Turks and as ragged as beggars. Our hair and beards were long, and we looked about as much like proper soldiers as a long-eared mule looks like a race horse.

To top it all, one morning we found water creeping slowly into our winter quarters. The flood gates to the old rice plantation nearby had been kept in repair so as to hold water out of the place, but I suppose they gave way. The water kept getting deeper and deeper. When the tide in the river fell, the water flowed off, but it came in again when the tide rose. So we had to move again, and received orders to get everything packed up.

Our regimental hospital steward had packed his tent and hospital supplies on his big mule, and tied him to a tree. The mule's load looked high as a hay stack but really was not so very heavy. All of a sudden the Rebs, who, I suppose, had seen us preparing to make some new move, began to throw big shells at us and oh, how they did shriek!

As the shells came, the big mule began to dance and jump and skip. Now the boys were always putting words and tune to some silly thing like that. So as a shell would come over, the boys would put words to the tune of the shell shriek, such as "Where is that mule, WHERE IS DAT MULE?" Pretty soon, a shell aimed lower than common struck a big tree, glanced down, and cut the rope that tied the mule. It passed right through his load and went on behind. As it came, someone says, "Where is that mule?" and as the shell struck his level another sings out, "Here he is, here is your mule." It was funny because it was not very dangerous. We soon moved back a few rods onto higher ground.

During this time, we had no boats with us. Rebel boats did pass up the river, though. Some of the boys captured an old flat boat loaded with cotton and a few provisions. Finally a battery was placed on the river bank with orders to stop all boats going up the river channel.

About the seventeenth of December, 1864, we finally received word that Fort McAllister had been captured by General Hazen, and we would soon have rations and clothes. We were told to put in requisitions for what clothes we *must* have, but to draw as light as possible because there were so many to be clothed.

You can imagine what a cheer went up from us. The Rebs heard us and sung out, "Say, Yanks, what you'uns yelling about, have you got orders to quit and go home?" We replied, "No," but that Lee had surrendered to Grant and we would eat them up tomorrow. Of course this lie of ours had no more effect on them than their lies had had on us.

At last we saw wagons coming up from the fleet— but they *were not for us!* They passed our camp and kept going. I well remember how we gathered together and consulted whether we should make a raid on the wagons and get something to eat. But we decided that as they were not guarded, it would be no fun, and so we gave up the idea. We soon got about half rations, not enough, but a help.

Meanwhile our bridge had been finished, along with another one just to our right. On the night of December twentieth, we received orders to be ready to march the next day at daylight. We were to take

sixty rounds of ammunition apiece and advance in
three columns across the swamp or canal, and drive
the Rebels from their works. One column would
cross on each of the two bridges we built, and one
directly across on the turnpike.

We had known what the bridges were being built
for, but had hoped that the city would surrender and
that we would not have to charge. When you consider
how few of us could stand abreast on these bridges
and roads, and how many guns and how much infantry could be massed against our front, each concen-
trating their fire on about sixty feet of road, you can
see that our task was very dangerous. How little sleep
there was in our camp that night! It seemed impossible to us that we *could* carry those works, especially
with such a thin line going against them. Men went
from tent to tent, and from company to company,
shaking hands with their friends and sending word by
them to the folks at home. Time and again, you
would hear it: "If you come out of this and I don't,
tell father—or mother—or my wife—or so-and-so—that
I thought of them tonight. If I am killed, give them
my watch as a keepsake." The answer always was:
"Yes, old boy, and if you come through all right and
I don't, do the same for me, and God Bless You!"

Our brigade was to lead the way across the turnpike, the worst place in the whole charge though none
of us mentioned it to one another. Once across the
turnpike bridge, we were to form in line and charge.

Well, the next morning, December twenty-first,
1864, we were up before daylight and formed in line
awaiting the command to march. Our canteens were

Scene at the crossing of a stream on an improvised bridge

filled. No one said much. It began to get daylight, yet
we got no orders to move. It got red in the east; still
no orders to move.

Way off to our right, we heard firing and cheers.
Then to our left, up by the river, we heard cheers.
Finally we moved out toward the road. Our regiment
was the second one in column. As the advance struck
the road, and filed down it toward the enemy, we held
our breath listening for the big guns and the little
guns and musketry that would just wipe them out of
this world.

But we heard no firing. As we struck the road and
turned down it, we could see the advance regiment
marching with flags floating and bayonets fixed right
up to the bridge. Our flag was flying, too. We thought
the Rebs were waiting until the road got packed, and
then would blow us all to Kingdom Come with their
artillery.

"What are they waiting for?" someone says nerv-
ously. Reply: "You'll hear from them in a minute."
All this time we marched ahead, and could see the
mouths of those big guns getting bigger and bigger.

The advance being by now quite close to the Rebel
works, a few men dashed forward, jumped up on the
works, and yelled like mad. They waved their hats
and yelled some more.

The Rebels had evacuated the works and left the
city during the night. Being unable to take their big
guns with them, they had left them behind to scare us.

Well, every man drew a long breath and then threw
up his ragged old cap in the air and yelled and yelled
again. It was, I imagine, like a man under sentence

of death receiving a reprieve. I often wonder, yet, how many of us would have been left alive if the Rebs had stayed there and fought as we expected.

But in spite of Sherman's having penned them up in their works, as he thought, they slipped across the river to South Carolina to fight another day. We went into camp without marching into the city. As the foragers went in to get some gruel for the boys, the citizens of Savannah tried the yellow-flag dodge on us. But we knew all about it, and searched for forage anyhow.

Orders had been issued beforehand that when the city fell, there was to be no pillaging and no plundering. By noon, the provost marshal's guards were patrolling the city. They permitted no stealing, not even of provisions. But of course, much of it was done when they were not looking. The boys were not much afraid of the guards, for when there were no officers in sight, the guards never molested the boys unless the boys got to stealing something more than provisions and that seldom happened.

About daylight one morning, several of us were walking down by the wharves when we heard a little artillery firing down the river, toward the ocean. Pretty soon we saw a black smoke coming up the river. We waited. Just about sunrise, there steamed up to the wharves a Rebel blockade runner. The captain did not know that the city had surrendered, and thought he was bringing relief to the city. He had run right past our fleet, which fired at him.

When the captain discovered his mistake, I never saw anyone look more ashamed and crest-fallen and

sorry than he did. The provost guards took possession
of his ship and turned her over to the proper authorities. He had come to the right place at the wrong
time, sad fate.

Bill and I while walking along the wharves came
across an Irish woman who was selling whiskey to the
boys at a dollar a drink. She asked us to buy. Bill said
he had no money. I said I had some Confederate
money. "That's what I want," says she. So Bill and I
took a drink.* I gave her a Confederate bill, and she
gave me change in Yankee money.

Bill and I then met several other boys uptown. In
passing a restaurant with a sign, "Meals at all hours,"
Bill says: "Bob, that money you have left will never
do you any more good than to use it right now to treat
us boys to a dinner." So we went in and inquired the
price of dinner.

The woman who ran the restaurant asked right off
whether we would pay her in Confederate or U.S.
money. I told her either one. She wanted no Confederate money, said she would give us a dinner for 75
cents U.S. although she did not have much in the
house to eat. We told her to get whatever she had,
quick. She served us some sort of soup, beans, bacon,
cornbread and molasses, and coffee made out of
parched beans. It tasted good to us, and we filled up
on it.

All the while, the woman seemed to think we

---

* Editor's note: Young Strong began his march across Georgia
as a teetotaler, but apparently learned to drink somewhere along
the way.

would not pay her, and acted afraid of us. She stared at us as if we were wild animals, but when we behaved ourselves properly, used decent language, and paid her as agreed, she seemed to conclude that maybe Yankees were not so very bad after all.

Becoming chatty, she told us of some of the hardships of the Savannah citizens. She told us how they had to make their own shoes and showed us a pair, the soles made of old boot tops and the uppers from heavy brown cloth carded and spun and woven by herself and her daughter. Everything in the house that was new was homemade.

One Sunday while in Savannah, a number of us attended church. The church was full, with a good many citizens and a great many soldiers. It was a fashionable church with ushers. These at first paid no attention to us and did not show us to seats. The minister in the opening prayer made no allusion to us or to the fall of the city, which was all right with us. But then he prayed for "the success of our arms"—meaning the Rebel arms—and that "the health and life of our President be preserved"—meaning Jeff Davis.

A member of our company who was sitting near the pulpit wrote a short note which he handed to an usher, and directed the usher to give it to the minister and ask him to read it immediately. The note directed the minister to pray for the President of the United States and for *all* in power, and added that he must do this without comment, and continue to do so at every service while we remained in the city. He was told that while we were not professors of religion, we were in the service of Abe Lincoln, Sherman, and Grant, and they must be prayed for and given equal showing with Davis, Lee, and the others.

That minister was smart enough for us. At the close of his sermon, he said: "We are taught in Holy Writ to pray for our *enemies.*" He then put up a powerful prayer that "the life of the President of the United States may be spared to the close of this cruel war, in order that his eyes may be opened to the right"; that Sherman, who commanded the Federal troops then in the city, "may be as merciful and wise in the government of the city as he has been successful in waging a devastating war," and so on.

When the minister stepped down from the pulpit, we shook hands with him and told him we had no more to say.

We had expected to be allowed to celebrate Christmas, but on the night of the twenty-fourth I was detailed as picket. We were sent two miles from the city to guard a certain road and the countryside around it. All the pickets were mad and vowed to be revenged. So about nine o'clock that night, we began firing. Of course the reserve came up to us on the run, and *their* reserve came up to them. It was pouring rain and all got wet. The officers blamed us for raising a false alarm, but when we thought the reserve had returned to their quarters and started fires to dry by, we began to fire off our guns all along the line and, of course, out and up through the rain came the reserve again. We did this two or three times, until the officers in charge begged us not to do it again. The officers said that if we would keep quiet, they would send us some punch for dinner. So we let them sleep.

The punch came about daylight and we filled up on it. Then we were ready for more mischief. If a local citizen tried to pass through our lines, we assured him our orders were to hang everyone who tried to get through without a pass. We actually did make a line of several gunslings and pass it around the necks of a great many. But, keeping one or two as hostages, we let most of them go after they promised to send us some dinner and whiskey.

By this time, a report had gotten to headquarters of what we were doing. Other troops were sent out to take our places and we were taken to camp and threatened with court-martial. But as we had done nothing very bad, and everything just in fun, we were allowed to go with only a reprimand.

We did not know how long we would remain there in camp, so we built us huts and real good ones, too, with fireplaces and bunks. We finished them on the next-to-last night of the year, and the next morning we received marching orders. We were moved to Hutchinson's Island, in the middle of the Savannah River, to guard a pontoon bridge. Just as we left our huts, another brigade moved in.

We went onto the island, but for some reason were ordered back that night. It had rained all day. We were wet through and cold, and had no wood to make fires. Someone had blundered, and we had to suffer for it.

After we got back, we were marched just in front of our huts that we had built and left the day before, and ordered to make camp. We asked permission of the boys occupying our huts to double up with them that night. They laughed at us and said these were their quarters, and they were going to keep them. Meantime our officers had gone off and found shelter in some house. Standing in the rain and mud, we held council of war and vowed to occupy our huts. So we fixed bayonets and advanced upon the huts. Taking their occupants by surprise, we threw them out into the rain and threw their guns and blankets after them.

Fussing like wet hens, they reported us to their officers, who reported us to *our* officers. Our officers refused to do anything, so they then reported us to division headquarters. But for some reason we were not disturbed, and stayed there all night. This was New Year's Eve, and I suppose you could say we celebrated it in our own fashion.

The next morning, January first, we were again ordered onto Hutchinson's Island, at that season one of the most miserable places I ever have been. The island was as bare of timber as a prairie, except for a fringe of big trees at the water's edge. It was sleeting and cold, and there we were with no wood for fuel or for our tents.*

We camped in the mud and rainwater puddles, with the sleet falling and freezing on our blankets. Al-

* Editor's note: The Civil War shelter halves or pup tents were issued without collapsible poles of any kind. To pitch the tents, soldiers cut two Y-shaped branches or saplings one-and-a-half to three inches in diameter, then cut a ridge pole to support the tent. Ends of the ridge pole rested in the Y-shaped poles. Being bare except for big timber, Hutchinson's Island afforded no such poles.

though I had by this time gotten pretty well used to *anything*, I remember that night as one of the worst I ever passed. The wind blew a hurricane and we had no shelter from it or anything else—not even rocks to lie on and keep us up out of the slush. You have seen rain, sleet, and mud form a slush. It was just such a bed we had that night.

The next morning, we got axes and cut enough of the big trees to make bonfires to dry us by. The Rebs just across the river on the South Carolina side kept shooting at us all day. One of our men who had climbed a tree to get a better sight of the country across the river was shot through the body and fell to the ground.

During the day, we finally learned what we were doing on the island in the first place. We were *holding it*, sitting and *waiting*. The engineers and bridge builders had been ordered to put a pontoon bridge across the channel on the far side of the island, to South Carolina, but on account of an unfavorable tide and of the Rebel sharpshooters, they failed to do it for a day or two.

There were at this time but comparatively few Rebs in our front, just across the river. This encouraged a number of us to cross in a skiff with General Harrison, who had been our colonel. I remember I was the only one from my company and regiment; all the rest in the skiff were strangers to me.

As it was several days before the main body of the army crossed, we slipped over unnoticed and had an easy time of it. I recall how the sun came out, and I lay down on some boards on the south side of an old

building to try and warm. Then I went back apiece
from the river to a house to get something to eat. I
kept wondering how many Johnnies might be there,
and whether they would get me, but I found no one
there but some niggers. They gave me a "hoe cake"
and I ate it.

After gorging on seafood and supplies brought in by way of the Atlantic and Savannah River, the Bluecoats moved on. To the surprise of most of them, they turned sharp left across the river and into South Carolina, marching at right angles to their former course. The route soon took them to Columbia, the state capital.

we head through south carolina

THE REST of my regiment finally got across the Savannah River on old flat boats which they rowed and poled over. I guess the engineers were still waiting for the right tide to build the pontoon bridge. We couldn't wait.

Once in South Carolina, we formed up and marched eight or nine miles into the state to a farmhouse belonging to the Rebel General Hardee—him who was the author of a military book known as *Hades' Tactics.** His tactics as taught in this book

* Editor's note: Strong here refers to *Hardee's Light Infantry Tactics for the U.S. Army,* a manual later adopted for Confederate use. William J. Hardee was born at Savannah in 1815, graduated from West Point in 1838, and served with distinction in the Mexican War, 1846–48. He became a Confederate colonel

were used by United States troops, Hardee having
been a United States officer before the war.

We lay at Hardee's farm some days to receive re-
cruits from back home and perhaps to reclothe, although I don't remember of drawing any clothing
there. Our duty consisted of camp guard, picket, and
helping to get teams, rations, and ammunition across
the river.

To go to the city of Savannah ourselves, we had to
pass down a canal built to irrigate Hardee's farm,
which was a rice farm; cross one stream or channel of
the river; cross Hutchinson's Island, then go by boat
or later by pontoon bridge to the city.

The weather was more wet than dry, and camp life
with its everlasting drill was very monotonous and
dull after the excitement and freedom of our late
march. There were no white people in the vicinity
except our soldiers and occasionally an overseer of
niggers.

One day while foraging we came to a plantation de-
serted by all except niggers and dogs. A number of
the nigs were winnowing rice. They had threshed it
first. Then taking a huge, low flat-bottomed basket
full of rice on their heads, they tipped it up and gave
it a slightly tremulous motion with their heads. This
allowed the rice to fall into another basket. They
repeated this process until the rice was clean of husks
and the like.

The dogs here were let out at us, and came snap-

---

at the start of the Civil War, rose to lieutenant general, and
commanded the defense of his native Savannah against Sherman—and Strong—in December, 1864. He owned land in South
Carolina near Hardeeville.

General William T. Sherman

"Sherman's March To The Sea"—engraving by Ritchie

General Sherman and his staff

A Yankee pontoon bridge

City of Savannah, Georgia

General Joseph Eggleston Johnston

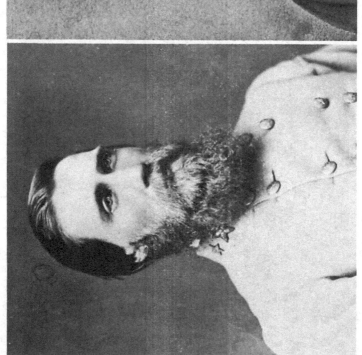

General John Bell Hood

The Capitol at Columbia, South Carolina

View of Columbia from the Capitol

General William T. Sherman and his staff at war's end

ping and snarling. Out of spite, we began shooting them. An old, gray-haired nig ran out with uplifted hands. He begged us not to shoot the dogs "as de fire scare my old woman powerful bad." Then he asked, "Is any of you a doctor?"

"Yes," says Mark Naper, pointing to me. "This man is a doctor."

"For Gawd's sake, Massa, come see my ole woman."

I promptly said I was no doctor, but Mark and the boys kept declaring I was. They said, "Now doc, what is the use of your being so proud—go and see the poor woman."

The old nigger believed all of them, not me, of course, and he begged and begged. The nigger women came out and begged, "Oh, fah de Lawd's sake, doctor, do come or Polly will die!" So finally I went in. I had not had enough sense to ask beforehand what the matter was. Now, behold, I found Polly in the pains of childbirth. I knew I had no business there, and left and coaxed the boys off before they had any idea of the woman's ailment. However little the nigs knew, they could do better for poor Polly than I.

We went on to forage the country wherever we could but found very little provisions.

One nice piece of eating I do remember. A number of the boys were detailed to go to the coast with wagons for oysters. When they came back, two or three wagons unloaded just in front of our company. We built a fire, threw a lot of the oysters on the fire, so roasted them, and ate until we filled up. We really had a feast.

I don't remember the date of our start through

Carolina, but our preparations were the same as when
we started from Atlanta. All sick and feeble men
were put into the hospital. Each able man received
a few days' rations. As usual, our orders to march
came a day to two before we were ready.

We did not march the very next day, and in the
morning I was sent on picket. Instead of being relieved later by our own troops, we were relieved by
other troops that took our places and were ordered
to report to our respective regiments. As we went to
camp, we found troops lining the road, all in motion.
Our regiment had the rearguard and were the last
to move out of camp.

We marched first in a northeast direction and then
nearly east, burning railroads and all public property
as we went, and living off the country. We had become expert foragers by this time. By watching all
fresh earth and probing with our bayonets, we usually
managed to find something.

I remember this part of South Carolina as low,
swampy, sandy country. It was here that the sweet
potato started from the ground. Here they took the
green sugar cane, laid it down, and covered it with
earth, and from the joints new sprouts started. They
made molasses from the cane juice or syrup. We
found barrels of molasses, carefully buried from us.
We would take what we wanted and usually leave
the rest.

When we entered South Carolina, a regular detail
was made up of foragers, to do this and nothing else
except in case of a battle. There were two squads,
alternating. One squad would forage for a day, while
the other remained with the regiment. Next day, the

other would go out while the first stayed with the regiment.

We were permitted to procure horses for ourselves, as we usually had long trips to make to find forage. At first, for a time, my steed was a raw-boned gray horse. I exchanged him one day with a citizen for a little bay mare that could almost outrun the wind.

More than once, I stayed behind the other foragers and the citizens and Reb soldiers chased me. But I don't remember but one time when I thought they would catch me.

We had been out after forage and found it. Loading up, we started back for camp. Just then, I saw a hog in a field. So I rode over, shot the hog, proceeded to skin the hams, and left the rest. By the time I got my hams tied to my saddle, the other boys were out of sight. Pretty soon, as I rode along, I heard firing in front. I supposed bushwhackers had attacked my comrades, but did not know how many of them there were nor whether they were between me and my comrades, or beyond them. So I went toward them, keeping a sharp lookout every foot of the way. Soon the firing ceased. Almost as soon as it stopped, I heard and saw a squad of Rebel cavalry coming down the road. I had no time to hide, so turned my mare and put her into a run.

The Rebs saw me and gave chase, shouting, "Surrender, you damned Yank!" I knew that if they caught me with my forage on me, they would kill me. So I lay as low on my mare's neck as I could and cut the hams from the saddle. Then I threw away my other forage.

The bullets zipped all around me. It was "Halt!"—

bang—"Surrender!"—bang. All this time, I was riding away from our boys and our lines. It was only a question of time, if I kept on as I was going, before I would run into more Rebs and more trouble.

While pounding along, I happened to think that some of the niggers around camp had said that my mare was a trained fox hunter. If she was, she was of course trained to jump. I determined to try her. I was going down a rail-fenced road. If I could get off it of a sudden, I could turn and shake off the Rebs.

I had no time to dismount and throw the top rail off the fence, for the Rebs were right behind me, shooting and yelping. It was sport to them, but not to me. I had often helped chase Rebs, just as I was being chased, and I knew how they felt—except that in my case capture spelled certain death because I was foraging. Suddenly on my right, a gun went off and a bullet whizzed by me. It meant more Rebs coming from that way.

I galloped a little farther, slowed up a little, straightened up in the saddle and lifted on the bit, and headed for the fence. That little mare jumped the fence as easy as I could a rail. Then I took off my hat, waved it at the Rebs, and rode off into the woods.

Yet they kept on. They fired at me, threw down the fence and came after me. Pretty soon I struck a sort of trail, going the way I wanted to go. I took it with the Rebs still after me, some shooting, some shouting "Surrender!" and one sport yelling, "Go it, Yank!" You may be sure I took his advice and went it.

By this time, I had run four or five miles and the mare was breathing pretty hard, but the Rebs had run just as far and maybe farther, and now I was getting nearer friends. I struck a road leading right toward our main column, which I guessed was about three miles off. I was sure my comrades were ahead of me.

Then I came to a creek that had a burned bridge across it. A tree had been felled across for a foot bridge, but I did not know how deep the creek was. So I slipped the bridle rein over the mare's head and coaxed her into the water. She did not want to go in. The Rebs were getting nearer all the time. I was just on the point of turning her loose and running for it when she jumped in and swam across. I mounted on the other shore and rode on. Soon I overtook the boys and was safe.

I remember how I petted that mare and how I wished I could send her North. Later on—oh, sad story—I lost her, not to the Rebs but to General Judson Kilpatrick's Cavalry. They seized all our Bummers' horses for cavalry remounts. I could have fought them.

Something happened about this time to prove to us that the danger to foragers was very real, not imagined. We had marched for days in low, swampy country with constant rains, mud over our shoetops, and streams overflowing. We came to a river that was swollen too deep and too wide to ford, so we moved back and camped on higher ground until our pontoons could be laid across the river.

Our foragers—my squad was not among them that time—had been ordered to meet us on the *other* side of the river. As we did not cross, we had of course to go to bed hungry. But that was not the worst of it. As there were none of our troops on the far side of the river, it left our foragers there in danger of being captured and killed by the enemy. Late that night, some of them came over, swimming their horses and bringing forage. They reported most were still on the other side.

The next morning, it was my squad's turn. I mounted my mare and with some others swam the river to get forage for the day. We had not gone two miles before we found two of the previous foraging party hanging to a tree. They were strung up by gun slings. They had been partially stripped, perhaps in a search. Their throats were cut and pinned to their drawers was a piece of paper with the words, "Death to all foragers," written on it.

We cut them down and laid them by the side of the road, leaving a guard to watch their bodies until our troops should come along. Our orders were to treat citizens with respect, but if our men were fired on by citizens or bushwhackers, to arrest all men within five miles and to burn all houses near the murder. We did it this day, telling the people why we did it. That night, we turned over a number of citizens as prisoners to the provost's guards. I don't know what was done with them, but suppose they were turned loose after swearing they knew nothing of the murders.

As we got a little farther north and east, the land got a little higher and we found better farms and farmhouses. One day four of us foragers from different regiments, who had become scattered from our own crowds, found ourselves at a little house. There were a number of white women there, but no men nor niggers. We found no forage, as other bummers had been there ahead of us. The women claimed to be Union people.

About a mile beyond, the women told us, was a house that no bummers had been to, at least from their direction. They said it was a big plantation house occupied by strong Rebels. We tried to find out if what they were telling us was to trap us, but concluded they were telling the truth, so we went on up to the big house.

One rode ahead to prevent surprise, two came along together, one brought up the rear. As there was only four of us it was very risky. I took the lead. When I got nearly to the house, I halted and looked all around carefully. I could see no one, so I motioned the boys to come up. When they came up, we put our horses to the run and dashed up to the house with our guns ready to fire if needed.

"Here come de Yankees, here come de Yankees!" the niggers hollered. The white children screamed. The niggers said, "De Yankees ain't got horns, dey is just like white folks!"

We found that we were the first Yankees ever seen by any of them, white or black. The mistress of the house, although badly scared and white as a sheet, bade us good evening and said, "Alight, gentlemen, alight." We let the niggers hold our horses in order have them ready at any minute. Then we told the lady she need not be alarmed as she would not be harmed in any way, but that we had to search the house for stragglers from the Rebel army and also for forage for ourselves.

Leaving one man to guard our horses, we searched for Rebs. We found none, but if we had been thieves we could have taken plenty of stuff. Evidently they did not expect us so far from our lines, and had hidden nothing. There were gold watches, rings, earrings, jewelry caskets, breast pins, and so on, but as we had no use for them we took none. I did take a straw hat.

Going outside, we confiscated a mule and loaded him up with provisions. The lady and her little children gathered on the porch as we left. She asked us if we were a fair sample of Yankee soldiers. We said, "Yes," of course. "Oh, such stories as we hear about Yankees every day," she said. "We were told that you were worse than brutes, that you insulted all women, burned all houses. Even though I didn't quite believe it, the children did. That is why they screamed when you came. We were told that you had horns, and stole everything."

The lady added that we treated her family better than some of Joe Wheeler's Rebel Cavalry did. We then advised her to hide her jewelry and most of her provisions, as other Yankees might not be as gentle as we had been. We explained that there were bad men in every crowd, and if the bad ones should come, they might rob her. But we assured her that she and her children need fear no personal harm or injury even from the worst of them.

By then, we had loaded our borrowed mule. We returned by the same little house first mentioned. It

Foraging in Georgia

was after sundown by this time. As travelling by night was dangerous, we camped down in the yard of the house. After all, there was no men there to inform the Rebs on us, and besides, we were as safe there as anywhere else outside our camp.

The women at the house claimed to have nothing to eat, so we divided with them and they cooked our supper. That night, two of us stood guard while two slept. In the morning, we gave the women a ham and some meal, telling them to hide it. Before we reached camp, we picked up another mule, set of harness, and a big family carriage. We loaded it up and made a nigger drive it to camp for us.

One day we fought a little war of our own over a grist mill. While foraging, we came upon the mill, built on a god-sized stream at a crossroads. In the mill was lots of corn. We had some niggers with us, so we set them to grinding the corn. There was fifteen to thirty of us, and we posted a guard over the mill while the rest of us hunted forage. After a while, all returned to the mill, fed our horses and ourselves, and relieved the guard. Then some slept and some fished while waiting for our grist.

All at once the guard shouted, "Here they come—fall in!" and began firing. Someone returned the fire. A squad of Rebs was upon us. The fishers dropped their lines and caught up their guns. As we did not know how many attackers there were, we mounted and left. The Rebs took possession of the mill.

After we had ridden a short distance, we dismounted, left a guard with the horses, and crept back and opened fire on the Rebs. They ran, and we took charge of the mill, and sent back for our horses. After a bit, the Rebs rallied and drove us out again. *Each party meanwhile kept the millers at work.*

Next we captured the mill again. This time we filled what sacks we could find, put them on our horses, and the next time the Rebs charged us we left for our camp.

Every big war consists of many little wars. Small-scale fighting ranged far and wide as Sherman's troops pushed northward through the Carolinas. Foragers, in particular, found themselves in constant peril from local surprise attacks. Strong several times had to fight for dear life.

 # war continues to be hell

THE BUMMERS had good luck at first in the interior of South Carolina and we seldom went hungry. The right flank of our army made excursions to the coast, and we of the left flank had it comparatively easy for a time. One day, however, we were hurried along a little faster and farther than common.

We heard firing in the front and left, and knew that General Kilpatrick and his cavalry were having a brush with Wheeler's Rebel Cavalry. That, however, was the cavalry's business. We went into camp as usual that night, just at sundown. We had just got our tents up and fires started when a mounted courier came dashing along, his horse all foam. As he rushed past, he yells: "Hold on, boys, don't unpack. Old Kilpatrick is in trouble."

We knew what that meant, and hurried to get a bite to eat. In a few minutes, a bugle sounded "Attention." We all listened to hear the next call, as we would know from it what troops were wanted. In a minute, our bugle sounded our call—which as I have said before was the first bar of "Hail Columbia"— followed instantly by the call to "Fall in." We were all ready. By the time Colonel Dustin came along with his horse on a run, we had formed a line.

Our bugle sounded, "Forward, double-quick march!" and away we went on the run. All in less time than it takes me now to draw my boot on. As we ran, word came back along the line that "Old Kil" had been attacked by a large force of Rebels. By this time, the firing was getting nearer. Soon we could hear the rattle of musketry mixed with the roar of artillery. In a few minutes more, we could hear the Rebel yell. We could distinguish the difference between the heavy roar of the Rebel musketry and the sharp crack of the Yankee cavalry carbines. By this time, we had run four or five miles and were getting short of wind.

When we heard a fresh Rebel yell, an increased roar of carbines, and almost instantly a wild Union cheer, we knew what it all meant just as well as if we had seen it, and we slacked our speed to a walk. The Rebs had made another charge on Kilpatrick—that was the yells—and when the Yanks cheered, that meant the charge had been repulsed. When we reached them, we found the Rebs, after their last charge had been repulsed, had pulled out and left. So after a short rest we returned to our camp. This occurred often, but I remember this particular time because we had to leave our supper.

We made another hard day's march next day. All day, it was rumored that we must be in Columbia, the capital of the state of South Carolina, before night. Columbia is situated where two rivers join, and all the bridges had been burned by the Rebs to keep us from crossing. Therefore we were much delayed and did not cross that day. If we could have crossed, I don't see what would have kept us from capturing Wheeler's Cavalry there, but we could not get over until pontoon bridges were laid later on.

Sometime before 4 P.M., we halted opposite the city. It was earlier than four because it was before sunset in the month of February. The stream was fifty to sixty rods wide. We could see the Rebels across it, with several pieces of artillery pointing towards our camp. They did not use them, thinking most likely that if they fired we would shell the city in retaliation.

The Rebel pickets came down to the riverside. Ours were stationed at the river bank on our side, so all were in plain sight. Our boys went to the river for water. The cavalry and artillery took their horses down, too, to drink. We called across to the Rebs not to run away during the night, as we would be over to visit them in the morning. They said they "reckoned" they could not spare the time to wait for us, because Lee wanted them in Virginia to run Grant off and that was more important.

Early in the morning, we were sent to the left, upstream, to where a pontoon had been laid in the night. The idea was to get beyond the city and intercept the Rebs when they left it. I, with the other bummers, was sent across this same pontoon. Our orders were to scout the country carefully and report any large bodies of Rebs we might find.

As we infantry bummers came up to the bridge, we found General Kilpatrick with his cavalry guarding it. He dismounted us and took our horses for his cavalry. I lost my good mare. Of course, our boys begged for their horses and used some swear words, but it availed naught. The cavalry *must* have horses, he says, and took them.

I crossed the pontoon on foot, about the first one of our squad over. Just after I passed over, I saw a log hut and went in. There was a cavalryman, trying to get something to eat. "Come now," he says to me, "There ain't enough grub here for two. You go on and let me alone." I had noticed his horse tied out in back, so I said, "I will go back and look in the chicken coop." I went out back, mounted his horse, and rode off. The cavalry had taken my horse so I took his. I managed to keep it only a short time, however, before it was taken from me and returned to the cavalry.

A good many prisoners were released about this time from the Rebel prison at Columbia, and returned to our army. Also, scouts and couriers succeeded in getting through to our fleet on the coast, and we heard plenty of rumors concerning Grant, but nothing reliable. We did not even know where we were going. Some said to Charleston, some said to Kinston, North Carolina. We all knew our object was somehow to weaken the Confederacy, and if possible to draw troops from Richmond. We daily expected a fight, but all through this part of South Carolina had only alarms.*

By this time, it had gotten harder to procure forage. Finally we began to go hungry pretty often. When we found forage, we nearly always had to fight for it. After having to turn our mounts over to the cavalry, we went back to the old system, one horse or mule to a company to carry forage for us.

One day after leaving Columbia we came in sight of a log house. Captain Culver had charge of us that day, and he and I rushed up to the house to capture anybody in it. As we rushed up with a clatter and shout, we saw a horse tied there. A Reb ran out with a revolver in each hand and yelled, "Surrender, d—n you, surrender or I'll blow you to hell!" As we were two to his one, we only laughed at him. The captain says, "perhaps, my friend, you had better change your mind and do the surrendering yourself." The Johnnie looked at us, laid down his pistols, and said: "Well, under the circumstances, perhaps I had."

His sweetheart lived in the house and, thinking the Yanks would be delayed in reaching that area, he had called to see her. His girl and her mother came to the

---

* Editor's note: The Union strategy finally worked to the extent that part of Lee's army confronting Grant was transferred to the Carolinas under General Joseph E. Johnston. This army, grown quite sizeable, fought a major battle against Sherman's forces at Bentonville, North Carolina, March 19 (CK), 1865, and did not surrender until two weeks after Appomattox.

door, screaming and crying and begged us not to kill him. We assured them that his life was in no danger but we should have to keep him. We allowed him to bid them goodbye.

The captain told me to take charge of the prisoner, and said he would hold me responsible for him. The others had come up to us by then, so while they hunted rations, he and I sat by the road. He was very chatty and pleasant, and told me all about his girl and about his mother, who lived nearby. As we became more sociable, he began to hint that I might let him go. How grateful, he suggested, his girl and his mother would be! Said one prisoner more or less would make no difference to our army, but it would make a vast difference to him and his.

"You know very well I can't let you go," I told him. "But if you want to take your chances, just start running. I am sorry for you, yet when you run, I must call out 'Halt!' and fire my gun at you. If you care to risk it, pull out."

He looked at me a minute, studying me carefully. Then he says: "That is an old trick. I have seen it done, and I don't believe I want to go."

I turned him over to the captain that night. Before we parted, he shook hands with me and asked me if I would have hit him, had he run. I told him, "No," but I would have had to shoot at him.

My next adventure came a few days later. I was not with the bummers that day, and they soon came in early without anything at all. They said the enemy cavalry were all around, thick as bees, and it was not safe to go even a mile from our column. They had made several attempts but had been driven back every time.

We had been living on short rations for a day or two, with very little before that, so the colonel sent the adjutant to each company to say that while he would not order out more foragers, he would allow six men from each company to volunteer to go. Six of us offered. Leaving our blankets and pup tents with the company, we took our one horse and started.

About a mile from camp, we came to a road that was just lined with bummers—infantry, cavalry, artillery and engineers—and all talking of the scarcity of forage. Away up the road, we could see a number of houses. We asked if these had been visited. All but one had, they said, and the Johnnies were holding that one when they went up there.

We of Company B held a consultation and agreed that because there were Rebs at this house an hour before, there was no reason for thinking they were there now. We offered to go reconnoiter. Soon we got into lower ground and could see nothing of our boys behind us or the farms ahead. Both sides of the road were lined with big trees but there was very little underbrush and no fences.

Suddenly some of our cavalry came down the road on the run. Their captain pulled up his horse long enough to ask us who we were and what we were up to. We told him. He said there was plenty of stuff at that big house, but the Johnnies were there and had just driven them back. He advised us to go back. Never have I seen a more demoralized set of men than these cavalrymen were. They were not in line, but came straggling along by ones and twos, each horse on the run. One had lost his hat, but did not stop for it. The Johnnies, they yelled, were right after them.

We waited to let them pass. Then we talked the matter over and concluded they were so badly scared that they did not know what they were doing. So we went on. Soon we met a lot of niggers. They said this place that we inquired about had lots of stuff in it, and no Yanks had been there. They added that the Rebs were there now. We asked, "How many?" They said, "The road is full of 'em."

Again we consulted and decided to go on. The sand was ankle deep or more, and walking was hard. All of a sudden, a squad of Rebs rode at us, horses on the run, "Surrender!" they yelled. In less than no time, we turned and ran toward our lines a mile away. *We ran!* The sand was deep, and we were just through a hard day's march. Soon we began to breathe hard.

I thought all the other boys were ahead of me, and I would surely be the sacrifice this time, when just behind me I heard a voice say: "For God's sake, Bob, don't leave me!" I looked over my shoulder and there was Bill Hughes coming sprinting behind me, throwing up the sand behind him each step.

"Allright," I says. "Jump behind a tree to the left and I'll take the right. Then you fire and fall back to another tree, and while you are loading I will fire at them."

Bill took a tree on one side, and I took one on the

other. He fired, and in half a minute I fired. Then he, then I. Every time we fired, we would fall back to another tree. We hoped they would think they had struck our picket line, and stop, and they did. Of course, we made all the noise we could, and they could not see how many of us there was.

Anyhow, the Rebs halted, deployed as skirmishers, and began firing. Thousands of bullets were fired at us two. It made such a racket that the boys back of us heard us. Our company boys begged of them to go out and save us. In a few minutes, here they came. They had no line, but were just a lot of Sherman's bummers. As they reached us, they formed a line. Someone yelled, "Forward, boys!" and forward we went.

We drove the Rebs back and back, and kept going. We found not only the one house, but plenty more where Yankees had not been, and we filled up our sacks, loaded our horse, and returned to camp. After the war, having moved to Nebraska, I didn't see Bill Hughes until one of my visits back home to Illinois. He was tickled to see me. Said I saved his life that time. Truly, I was as glad to stop as he was, for I was completely "run out." If we had taken a regular double-quick step, we could have run for miles, but the Rebs on horseback would have caught us.

In South Carolina niggers flocked to us, if possible, thicker than they did in Georgia. They came in droves, deserting the old plantations entirely in some instances. Often they brought wagon loads of stuff. Sometimes they had a yoke of oxen "geared" to the family carriage, and it full of nigger babies. They were a nuisance and a curse. They seemed to think that if they were only near "Massa Lincoln's men," they were safe from all earthly ills. We tried to drive them back, but very seldom succeeded. As forage become scarcer, they suffered many times for food. As in Georgia, they were not allowed to march in the road unless they kept to the rear, and that was sure capture for them. So they marched by the side of the road and through the fields.

Through this section of the South, the white people are great horseback riders, women and all. Many times while we were on the march, we would see parties of ladies sitting on their horses by the roadside watching the Yankees pass. Sometimes they were at a crossroad on a journey, and, finding the army passing, would halt for us to pass. Most likely they had to wait a long time, as we were always many hours passing any given point. They were never molested or spoken to unless they were quite near the road. Then such remarks as, "Good morning, honey," would be addressed to them.

The people of the South are great on using terms of endearment to the female sex. Then and now, "Honey" is a perfectly proper way to address anyone. A woman calls her husband and her children "Honey." The husband calls his wife, "Honey." Boys and girls call each other "Honey." It was and is all right. It is a national name. We just "caught on," and no offense meant.

The ladies usually wore a homespun and home-colored riding dress or skirt, and a huge sun bonnet with whale-bone or hickory splints to stiffen it. If

they remained quiet, no one went after them. But if
a woman or man rode rapidly away, they were followed to see what mischief they were up to. If anything suspicious was discovered, they were seized and
brought back to the commanding officer. As we were
always surrounded by spies, anyone in a haste to get
away from us always looked suspicious. Usually we
held them until the column passed. Then, if there
was no real evidence against them, they were let go.

Again, the war took a new turn. The strategy now was to crush Lee's Army of Northern Virginia between the two huge Union armies, the Army of the Potomac under Grant and Meade on one side, and Sherman's travel-weary troops on the other. Hood's Confederates had suffered a crippling defeat in Tennessee. Hastily the South returned command of that army to Johnston, who moved to intercept Sherman in North Carolina.

 # we fight our last big battle

AFTER GEORGIA with its red clay hills and swamps, and South Carolina with its swamps and sand, we found in North Carolina immense pitch pine forests. Sometimes for miles and miles there was nothing else. Pine cones and pine needles covered the ground. At noon and night halts, we would pelt each other with pine cones.

In the turpentine belt, we became as black as Guinea niggers. Pine knots and logs would burn in spite of rain, even, and would send up clouds of thick, black, oily, sooty smoke. The boys would surround the fire and the wind would blow this oily, sooty smoke into their faces. Nothing but soap and hot water would remove it, and as we had neither, we were a dirty set.

One thing we did as often as possible, even two or three times a day, was to hunt "gray backs." At a halt of any length, off would come our shirts and pants, and we would chase the festive louse in and out of seams. We called it "skirmishing," but do our best, we still could not keep them down. We had had for months no opportunity to boil our clothes and the vermin increased rapidly.

While marching through the turpentine region, we often came upon tar burners. The natives cut and piled great piles of logs, then covered them with earth, leaving a flue in the middle of the pile at top and a hole from the bottom for a draft. Also at the side was a hole where the dross escaped in a thick, black, steaming stinking stream, the residue being tar. I remember the first ones I saw, with thick black smoke rising up miles ahead of us. As we came nearer, the smoke seemed to rise from huge piles of earth. The wood was underneath, of course.

Before burning the logs to make tar, the people slashed the trees for turpentine. These trees, say forty to fifty feet tall and two to three feet in diameter, had on three sides of them little, shallow trenches cut into them. The lower cut or slash was made deeper and like a cup to hold the pitch as it exudes from the slanting cuts above. The pitch is then gathered in buckets and turpentine is distilled from it. It is after the pitch ceases to run that the trees are cut and burned for tar.

The people living in these North Carolina forests

are called Tar Heels. They did not like us because of one of our pranks. At night, we used to set fire to their tree trenches to see the trees burn. Often the fire would run up to the tops of the trees. The burning trees would seem to be dangerous, but I never knew anyone to be hurt by them.

When a tired soldier leaned against these trees to doze during a halt in the march, some fellow would be almost sure to set fire to these cups. Soon when the pitch got hot, it would run down the tree and glue the sleeper to the burning tree. Then the roaring fire above his head would wake him. His frantic efforts to get free would raise a laugh. When he got loose, he usually wanted to whip someone but never could find anyone to fight him. All would be laughing at the next victim, so he would begin to laugh too.

As we neared the city of Fayetteville, North Carolina, we were told to have our mail ready. A courier had brought word that a gunboat would be up the Cape Fear River there to take our mail, and that possibly boats would be up with rations and clothing. A gunboat did come up the river, but no transports with rations or clothing came.

The day Fayetteville was captured, I was out with the bummers. We received orders that morning to watch the enemy, but not to rush the city. We could see for miles in every direction. Our left wing of the army at this point consisted of two corps, the 14th and 20th. Foragers from both corps gathered on a high hill about two miles from the city. We could see the 14th Corps as they advanced and prepared to drive the Rebels out.

We judged by the Rebels' actions that they were

preparing to leave the city. Someone proposed that we throw out skirmishers and drive in the enemy's pickets from out side, and see if we could not beat the rest of the army into the city. So some of us formed a skirmish line, and the rest supported them, all ready for a rush. I suppose there was five hundred of us.

No doubt the Rebs expected the Yanks would attack with a strong force. Probably their scouts had reported the force on the west and southwest of the city, but we bummers were on the northwest. So we drove the Rebs without much trouble, being unexpected, and as they ran they reported an attack from our direction. They undoubtedly thought the city was nearly surrounded, and they left on the run.

We had a race with the 14th Corps, but we bummers got there first although that corps claims to have taken the city. They were, in truth, the first regular troops to enter the place. Anyhow, as many of the bummers belonged to the 14th as belonged to the 20th.

The roads around Fayetteville were in horrible condition. We lay in town two days to rest ourselves and the teams. When we set out over those roads, the teams some days would not make more than two miles. That gave us lots of work to do, building corduroy roads, which I have described, and pulling wagons out of the bottomless mud. Also, the situation gave us less territory to forage over than when we traveled fifteen or twenty miles a day.

One day in the foothills, we passed near what is called "the hanging rock." The rock sat just on the edge of a bluff or precipice. It was shaped something like an egg, and was so evenly balanced that one man could easily set it rocking. A dozen or more of us tried to roll it over the bluff, for the fun of it. We could rock it or swing it just about so far. Then back it would come, and we would have to move lively to get out of its way.

On the night of March 16, 1865, I think it was, we went into camp and received a report that General Johnston was in front of us with his whole army and intended to wipe us out on the morrow. That is what the prisoners we captured that day told us. We knew Johnston of old, from the hard fighting around Atlanta, and knew that if he was in front of us we had our work cut out for us. Still I don't believe we lost any sleep over it, as we had plenty of ground to move on. It was not like that night at Savannah, when we were penned up to a narrow bridge approach. I remember talking about it that night, and saying we were tired of marching and would be glad of a brush with the Rebs for a change. Yet we knew that the war must be about over, and we hated to think of being killed or wounded at this late date.

Sure enough, the next morning the bummers were ordered not to go out. Our whole regiment was thrown out as skirmishers and ordered to advance and drive the enemy pickets in. The pickets did not want to be driven, but we finally got them started.

The 105th, still in skirmish line, was then sent around to our left. First the bugle sounded, "By the left flank," then "forward." Joe Hammersmith was on the extreme left. When ordered to advance, he did not hear the call "forward" and kept going farther

and farther to the left until he ran into the Rebs by
himself and was captured. Joe wore a big silver watch
such as we used to call a "bull's eye." Later that day,
we captured a Reb who had a very familiar-looking
watch. We asked him how he came by it. He replied
they captured a Dutchman this morning, and the
Dutchman gave him the watch. We told him we knew
the watch and would take care of it for our comrade.
So we relieved him of it, and did so.

There was a Rebel battery that kept annoying us,
and about noon, we received orders to take that battery and be quick about it. At the time, I suppose we
were about forty rods from it, and it kept pouring
grape and canister into us. Two of our regiments
were ordered up, the 105th and I think the 129th. We
were told that Brigadier General Dustin, our old
colonel, who had been promoted and given another
command, was about to charge this same battery from
the right. So we wanted to get there first.

The battery was inside a fort. As we charged up to
it, they, of course, poured it into us *lively*. Just as we
started, we heard cheers on our right and knew that
Dustin and his men were racing for the guns. In three
minutes, we were over the fort works and the battery
was ours. We got there a minute before Dustin did.
The battery covered about as much ground as our
front yard. On that small piece of ground I counted
thirty-three dead Rebels and many wounded—and all
done in a few minutes' time. Whether they did not
have time to run or whether they would not run, I
do not know.

After capturing the battery, we advanced across the

road. Just in front of us there we found a line of entrenchments. Without charging them, we settled down to a quiet fight at short range. The Rebs were on just a little higher ground than we were. The ground was covered with an almost impenetrable thicket of young pines. By stooping, we could look under the pines and see the Rebs' legs.

We held them there—or rather, they held us there—until night. At that time, we lay down to sleep on the battlefield, having, of course, put out strong guards.

Next morning, I was detailed for the skirmish line, out in front of everybody. Just at sunrise, we skirmishers saw three men step out of the brush across an open field some sixty rods from us. One of them waved his hat and shouted at us, but he was so excited that we could not understand him. They would come towards us a little ways, then halt and wave the hat.

We shouted to them to come into our lines if they wanted to. We said we would not shoot, but they must either come in quick or get into the brush quick. We could not have them roaming between our lines and theirs. They came right in and proved to be deserters from the Rebels. They said their army had gone, but they hid until they saw us and then surrendered.

With the Rebel army withdrawn, we resumed our march. At this point, a change in the manner of our marching was ordered. It looked like the idea was to give our wagons better protection. We marched along three parallel roads: On the left, a division of troops of our 20th Corps without any wagons; on the center road, a brigade, then all the wagons, then the other

Union pickets approached by Confederates disguised
in cedar bushes

two brigades of that division; on the right, the other division of our corps without any wagons. Still farther to the right marched the 14th Corps in about the same order.

Early on the morning of March 19, 1865, we heard cannonading in front. As our brigade was in the middle of the center column, behind the wagons, we did not trouble ourselves much about it. The firing got heavier and heavier. About noon, a courier came dashing back, his horse all lather. He hung his head but kept on a run. The courier never halted at the head of our column, but shouted as he kept going, "Hurry up, boys, the Johnnies have got the First driven into a trap and are giving them Hell."

We knew what the next word would be, of course, and every man tightened his belt for a run. The courier had hardly passed us when our brigade bugle sounded: "Attention. Forward March, Double Quick!"

We actually ran eight miles without a halt. That is, some did. Some played out and fell down and were run over by the rest. They were left to recover their wind.

As we advanced, the sound of battle became plainer and nearer. It rained, then stopped and the sun began shining. As there was a slight hill in our front, we could see nothing. Soon, though, we could hear the yells of the Rebs as they charged our boys. Then the roar of artillery and rattle of musketry would increase. Then a loud and clear Yankee cheer would tell us that that charge had been repulsed.

Our fear was that the Rebs might break the Union

line before we could get there. In that case, it meant
for us either a fight at a disadvantage or a retreat. We
never had been driven from the field, but we knew
that if the Union line in front of us was broken and
the Rebs charged us while we were in marching column instead of line of battle, we would be at a great
disadvantage.

Soon the shells and bullets began to drop among
us. Then we reached the top of the hill and were
ordered into line of battle. We halted there, and just
below us was a *grand sight*. I can't quite describe it.

Just below us, at the bottom of a gentle slope in an
old field, the Yankee boys were lying down behind a
very slight breastwork that looked like it had been
thrown up in a hurry. Beyond them, the Rebels were
just coming out of the woods for a charge. They came
at a walk with bayonets fixed, while their officers rode
along in their front, waving their swords and cheering on the men.

Between the two armies stood the beautiful tents
of the Yankees. We could tell these were hospital
tents. They had established the hospital earlier in the
day, at what was then the rear. But now they had been
driven back until the hospital was between them and
the Rebs.

Our brigade was halted at the top of the slope until
a position could be chosen for us. The Second Brigade
of our division was ordered down the slope to meet
the Rebs. They went down on the run, cheering the
boys behind the breastworks. It was the first inkling
that the boys at the breastworks, or Rebs either, had
that we were within miles of them. I'll venture to say

that our boys would rather have seen us than draw a year's pay.

We of the First Brigade kept our position on the hill, standing still and looking at the fight, with the bullets whistling around us. This battle became known later as the Battle of Bentonville, as it was near that place in North Carolina. While we did not know it then, it was the last battle we were to be in.

Anyhow, it was the second battle I ever had a good chance to see, having nothing to do but look on. There we stood, not forty rods (about two hundred yards) to the rear, while the Rebs charged up to our line just in front of us.

The Rebs came at a walk until thirty or forty rods from our boys. Then their officers went to the rear and their bugles called "Charge!" For five minutes, everything was as quiet as death. To us in the rear the silence seemed *awful*. The Rebs lowered their guns to the position "charge," and started for our lines with a yell.

Our boys continued lying down. They remained as quiet as logs until the Rebs got so near that it seemed as if they would be run over. Suddenly, when the Rebs could not have been more than ten rods (165 feet) away, our bugles sounded "Rise up, Fire!"

We could see the smoke leap from our guns almost into the faces of the Rebs. They fired so fast that the smoke hid the Rebs from us.*

Just then, a staff officer dashed up on his horse. Major Brown, who was in command of our regiment,

* Editor's note: This suggests that the Federal troops were using Spencer repeaters instead of Springfield muzzleloaders.

yelled out: "Attention 105th, Forward, Double Quick March!" Away we went to the left of the boys who were fighting. As we started, we heard the Yankee cheer and knew the Reb charge was repulsed.

We now took position at the left of the boys. The order came through, "Ten volunteers for the skirmish line." I was among the volunteers. As we ten stepped to the front, the order was, "Skirmishers to the front and hold them." Then, "Battalion attention! Front rank, stand to your arms. Rear rank stack arms." While the front rank stood ready to repel any charge, the rear rank began to build breastworks.

We skirmishers meanwhile went out on the run some twenty or thirty rods ahead of the line, and of course, that much nearer the Rebels. Each one of us got behind a tree and tried to shoot a Rebel without being shot ourselves. The earlier fighting that day had been across an open field, but now we were in heavy timber with no underbrush. The trees were all large, and we could see quite a ways.

The skirmishers, being ahead of our line, would have to stand the first brunt of a charge. Rebel sharp-shooters would pay us plenty of attention while their lines were re-forming to charge. But as we could hide behind trees and protect ourselves, and had no hard work to do such as the boys in the line were doing, it was not such a bad place to be in after all. In case the Rebs charged us and we skirmishers could not check or stop them, we could fall back onto the line.

During this time, the boys in the line worked with spades and axes like beavers. The rear line would work a few minutes just as hard as they could. Then the front line changed places with them. In a little while, they had a splendid set of works built. It was said that in two hours, we had marched eight miles and put up a fine breastworks, so you can see that every boy ran hard and every boy worked hard. Those that had been outrun in the race to the battle began to come in and take their places in the ranks, going to work with the rest. The line of works that the boys built joined onto the line built earlier by the boys that had been fighting, but joined at an angle extending to the front, towards the Rebs.

The Rebs charged the works every half hour. They did not reach our brigade, but did reach some of the fresh troops on the angle. While on the skirmish line, I saw the Rebs make five different charges before dark. Each time, they came out of the woods in almost perfect alignment with guns at "shoulder arms." When they got about so close, their officers would retire behind the advance lines, the Rebs would drop their guns to a charge, and with yell after yell would dash forward.

Our boys in the line would wait until they were about so near. Then they would fire at them, scatter them, and back they would go. As they went back, our artillery and musketry would pour in fire amid cheer after cheer. Then as they got behind their artillery, it would open up on our boys. As soon as they came in sight of us skirmishers, we would pour our fire into them but they paid no more attention to us (firing from the flank) than if we had been so many flies. We would keep up our fire until they got back out of sight.

Every one of their charges was repulsed. We wondered then why they were so persistent when they could see that our reinforcements had arrived. From prisoners, we later found out why. They were trying to hold us there until other parts of their army could whip the Yanks in another part of the field. Then they would all turn on us and clean us out. They never managed it.

The Rebs remained in our front that night and the next day, without any further charges. They pulled out the second night, and we set out after them the next morning. That morning, it was rumored that we might meet up with another Yankee Army, led by General Schofield, which had fought its way up from the coast after capturing Wilmington. Sure enough, we soon saw troops standing in the road whose battle-flag was strange to us. As we passed them, the flag waved and cheers went up. They were part of Schofield's troops, welcoming us.*

The morning of the second day, soon after breaking camp, we passed a camp of nigger troops. They also cheered us of Sherman's Army. Almost immediately after passing the nigger troops, our bummers came in reporting a force of Rebs just ahead, behind some breastworks. We halted, and the usual orders were given. Just then, the officers of the nigger troops

---

* Editor's note: Major General J. M. Schofield made an independent advance into North Carolina from the coast. His forces included the Twenty-Third Corps, released from Tennessee by the defeat of Hood's Confederates there, and shipped around to Fort Risher, N. C. Schofield's forces captured Wilmington, N. C., February 22, 1865, then fanned out and took New Berne, Kinston and Goldsboro.

offered to charge the breastworks. This was agreeable to us, of course, so we stacked arms and let the black boys pile past us. They deployed in line of battle and went in with a rush and a roar, driving the Johnnies. That, I think, was the last armed force of Rebels I ever saw. Once later on, we started from Raleigh to clean out the remnant of Johnston's Army but he surrendered before we reached him. That is getting ahead of the story, however.

We marched to Goldsboro, North Carolina, where we remained some days. On arriving there, all foragers were ordered to turn over to the proper authority all horses and mules that they had been using. The best were kept for the artillery and cavalry and wagons, and the rest were turned loose to graze. Citizens who needed them and who could and did prove they did not want the animals for Confederate use were allowed to catch and keep them.

I learned that Cousin Henry Strong's regiment was encamped with the other wing of the army and that the way was clear to them. So I procured a pass and permission to be gone all day. Just before dark, I went out and caught a horse. I had my pick among *thousands,* and I chose a light sorrel with only one eye. But he was clean-limbed and built like a greyhound. I tied him to my tent and begged some corn and hay from the quartermaster and fed him night and morning.

Henry's regiment was said to be thirty-five miles away. I started out one morning before daylight, taking with me my dinner of hardtack and bacon and a feed of corn for my horse. Well, that was the best horse I ever rode. He was tough as a knot. I rode hard for hours, and he never sweated a hair. I reached Henry's regiment and found that he had been made brigade teamster and was then away gathering forage for the brigade teams. So I did not see him, but had a fine ride and saw some fine country. When I got back, I turned my horse out to graze.

While at Goldsboro, we drew rations and clothing, also soap and big camp kettles, and proceeded to clean up. We not only took baths ourselves, but we boiled all our clothes, blankets, tent clothes, etc., to kill the festive louse. We lay at Goldsboro only a short time, but long enough to get rid of the niggers who had congregated around our camp and long enough to draw fresh ammunition.

We stayed at Goldsboro until, I think, April 7, 1865, when we were ordered to proceed to Raleigh to attack Johnston's Army. While we were marching near Smithfield, we saw, way ahead of us, hats being thrown in the air. Cheers and shouts went up. Pretty soon we were halted and then we could see a courier coming down the road. As he passed along, the boys seemed to go wild. When he reached the head of our regiment, our boys went wild, too. We at the rear could not hear what he said. As he reached us, he yelled: "Lee has surrendered!" He just kept that up all the time, as he rode along.

Well, perhaps you can imagine what that meant to us. It meant home, mother, father, brothers, and sisters, and to some it meant that *and* wife and children. To all it meant that the war would soon be over, and we hurrahed and yelled and threw up our hats. In a few minutes we were halted and stacked arms. Then we had a jubilee, shook hands with each other. Some turned somersaults and stood on their heads and clapped their feet together.

There soon came to each regiment commander an official notice with orders to read it to the men. We were formed in hollow squares and the order read to us. After stating that Lee had surrendered and that his soldiers had been paroled and sent home, the order cautioned us against any more foraging. We were requested to be careful in our intercourse with the citizens, and were ordered not to molest any Rebel soldiers we might find at their homes. We were told that as conquerors we could afford to be magnanimous.

Then we resumed our march, and arrived at Raleigh, North Carolina, and went into camp for some days. It was two days after this, I think, that we received the news of Lincoln's murder. Then we became *mad*. Strict orders had to be issued us to remain in our quarters at night.

At Raleigh we met a good many of Lee's veterans. At first they seemed timid and afraid that we might abuse them. I remember the morning before the Lincoln news, I was walking through the city and came to a yard. At the front gate stood a Rebel soldier. By his side was his wife, one hand on his shoulder, and two or three kids were hanging onto him. He was still dressed in Rebel uniform. As I approached the gate, he gave me a military salute which I returned and I bade them both good morning. He asked me if I was in a hurry. I said, "No." He and his wife then asked me into the yard, gave me a chair under a big tree, and he sat down with a child on each knee. His wife stood with her hand on his shoulder. We had a long talk. He asked me if he and other returning Rebels would be perfectly safe from molestations. I said I was sure they would be, but advised him to remain at home a few days or at least to avoid our camp.

Then came the news of Lincoln's murder, and for a day or two *the returned Rebels were not safe.* I called on this man and found him at home. His wife was badly scared. She thought every Southern soldier would be killed. He asked me if I still thought he was safe? I said, "Yes, if you don't get into any arguments with the Yankees." I told him everybody was mad, but would cool down if nothing fresh happened to stir them up.

Extra strong guards were put on over the camp, and nobody was allowed outside camp except under a strong guard to assure good conduct. But the great excitement wore off in a few days.

At Raleigh there was an asylum for the insane. Great crowds used to gather there to listen to the ravings of the crazy ones. The patients would crowd to the barred windows and talk with us or swear at us. One woman would perch herself on the window and after looking over the crowd and pointing at someone would say: "There is the man who sent me here! He is the father of my child. Bring him here and I will scratch his eyes out!"

One fine, portly man imagined himself the Supreme Head of the World, and kept enquiring the news. He called us his cousins, and would talk about the present war. He declared it must be stopped, as too many of his subjects were being killed. Sometimes he would ask, "Who commands *my troops* near here?" We would say, "General Sherman." He would say, "Tell General Sherman to treat the ladies gently and with courtesy." Then he would get mad and add, "Kill all the men!"

The crowd operated badly on the poor crazy people and we finally put a guard around the building. Some of the patients, we thought, were not crazy at all.

One young man in the asylum, son of a North Carolina planter, claimed to have been educated in a college in New York. While at school, he said, he fell in love with a New York girl, became engaged, and was to marry when he finished his studies. In the meantime, the war broke out. He was called home, and his father said no son of his should marry a Yankee. The son refused to enter the Rebel Army. He declared his intention of returning North, marrying the girl and entering the Union Army.

At that point his father, who was rich and influential, had him shut up in the asylum as if he were really crazy. There was New York battery along with us. Some of the boys in it had attended college with the young North Carolinian and they corroborated his story. Anyhow the story created so much interest among us that there were threats of pulling down the building to release him.

Finally Sherman himself became interested. Physicians were called to examine the boy. They pronounced him sane. He was released and joined the New York battery and marched north with us.

While marching north, through a town in the Carolinas, we saw Sherman in the town square seated on a block. As we passed, we saluted him and he us. Just behind him and at his left was an elevated platform surrounded by a railing. In the center of the platform was a tall, stout post with rings and cords attached to it. The platform was the auctioneer's stand where he knocked down niggers to the highest bidder. The post in the center was the whipping post.

Whether Sherman had just discovered what all of this was, or why he had not called it to the attention of the troops that had already passed, I don't know. But just as we came in front of him he cast his eyes toward this platform and waved his hand slightly at it. We got the idea. In just a minute, we had it torn down. Someone struck a match to it, and the block and whipping post were no more.

As we hurried by Sherman to regain our places in the line, which had not stopped, we asked him: "How's that, General?" He grinned and said, "Good job."

The surrender of Lee's and Johnston's Confederate armies meant no surcease in marching. Across the torn battlefields of Virginia, the blue columns tramped north to Washington in such intense heat that men collapsed and died. When the westerners at last made contact with the Army of the Potomac, there was sharp rivalry between "Sherman's mules" and the "featherbed" soldiers from the East.

our last long march proves a killer

I<small>T</small> W<small>AS</small> at or near Raleigh that General Sherman and Johnston arranged terms for Johnston's surrender. Sherman sent the terms to Washington for approval. They came back "disapproved,"* and he was ordered to renew hostilities. We were all mad, as we thought the war was over.

That night, our bugles sounded "Attention!" and then "Strike tents—Fall in—Forward march." We

* Editor's note: Sherman gave such generous terms to his old fellow West Pointer, Joseph E. Johnston, that the administration rejected them. Sherman would have let the Confederates march home to their state capitals *under arms* and stack arms there, without surrendering individually. Grant warned him this would never do. The final terms were like those at Appomattox earlier: Surrender all arms and give individual paroles.

marched with only quarter rations but with plenty of ammunition. We marched all night, halted in an old field for breakfast, then pulled out again and kept going. That night we camped near Johnston's Army, prepared to attack him. For two or three days, each army stayed there, right where it was. Neither army wanted to fight. We did no fighting, not even picket firing, as we knew that new terms of surrender were being prepared and we all wanted to go home.

No foraging was allowed during this time. In fact, there was nothing to forage. Between the two armies, the citizens were entirely cleaned out. On the third day, I think it was, the new terms were accepted and Johnston's Army was surrendered in form. Each Rebel was given a parole and furnished transportation home. Each was at liberty to catch a mule or horse and take it home with him, as long as the beasts lasted. Each was given a few days rations. Rations soon accumulated and were issued to the citizens. Between and among the armies, there was general and boisterous rejoicing.

We then returned to Raleigh and prepared for our final march, to Washington, D.C. Who was responsible for the severity of that march I don't know. General Joseph A. Mower had been placed in command of our corps and it was said that he and other corps commanders had laid wagers as to who would reach Washington first.

The first half of the march was not hard, but then began the race. By then, it was very hot in the South. The march we were on wore out the best of us. Men fell out by the roadside and lay there completely exhausted. Sometimes the captain, or if the captain fell out, some other officer who would be leading the company, would find he had only three or four men following him and would draw them to one side and all lay down to rest. Some nights when going into camp the colonel would not have fifty men in his regiment.

We had made many forced marches on our long, roundabout route from Louisville, Kentucky, through Tennessee, Georgia and the Carolinas, but *this* march after the war was over always makes me *mad* to think of, even now. I was tough then, and I don't remember as I fell out any time, but suppose I did.

I have seen men dying from exhaustion, lying in fence corners, whose deaths were simply murder. No one had time to wait on anyone, especially if he was a stranger. When our own boys fell down, we would pull them into the shade, pour water on their heads, and go on and leave them. We lost no men by death on this march, but we saw dead men lying in fence corners or under trees every day. After the first few days the boys got mad and fell out when they got tired. Then they came on when rested, and no rear guard meddled with them.

We marched through Richmond, Virginia, and by the famous Libby Prison. A large section of the city had been burned. For blocks and blocks, the weeds and grass were coming up between the paving stones and also growing where houses had been. It was a picture of desolation and ruin.

Orders here in this vicinity were very strict against all foraging, but it went on. The boys had innumerable excuses when found with a pig, goose or chicken. Some would claim that the geese tried to bite them and had to be killed in self-defense. Others had even better stories. Chickens would crow to the tune of Dixie, so had to be killed. Pigs squealed for Jeff Davis and the soldiers *could not stand that!* Sometimes a chicken or pig would not halt when ordered to do so, and therefore was "halted." Sometimes the animals refused to crow or grunt for General Sherman.

When we left Richmond, some of our hardest marching began. The weather was so hot, and we tramped along at three or four miles an hour day after day. We marched through the most beautiful scenery in Virginia. War had not completely devastated the country, and for days we passed through fine farms and thriving villages. The farms had fine large mansions and clusters of nigger huts, all whitewashed.

We passed over several battlegrounds. At the Battle of the Wilderness scene, we marched for hours over the battlefield. You know, the battle lasted several days and as the armies changed positions they covered much ground. We could tell by the graves where the Rebels and Yankees had stood. In one or two instances, could tell just how far the charges had gone. The dead had been buried where they fell, and the burial consisted only of throwing a little dirt over the dead men. Here and there an arm or leg or a hand or foot would stick out, and by the color of the uniform we knew which were Yanks and which were Rebs.

Dogs and hogs had in many cases unearthed bodies and dragged them several feet. Legs and arms were scattered around.

It seems terrible to think of now, but at that time the boys would kick a skull out of the way as indifferently as if it had been a stone. Someone would pick up a skull with a bullet hole in it and speculate about how the deceased got hit.

Right in the line of breastworks stood a lone house. When we passed the house, it was occupied only by women, not a single living man. They were surrounded by the bones of thousands of dead men. As we passed the door, one of our boys, Dick, had a skull in his hands. The women were crowded in the doorway. Dick, who had the skull, says to them: "Good morning, ladies. Did you have any friends in this fight here?"

"Yes," said one of them, "I had a brother killed."

"Here is his head," said Dick, and tossed the skull in among them. How heartless!

All along the line of our march white people and niggers flocked to the road to see us. The white ones were glad the war was over, but were depressed at the havoc done their homes. The niggers were jubilant and happy. They called us Massa Lincoln's men, and nothing in their power to do or get for us was too good for us to have.

Sergeant Mark Naper's place in the line of march was to the right. One evening just before dark as we were marching along we met crowds of niggers tramping down the road. We asked them where they were going. "Down to the dance." A fresh crowd came along, among them one wench not very old, but, oh, so big and fat and greasy. We must have been the first Yankees she had seen, for she stopped, threw up her hands, and says, "Bress de Lawd, is you Massa Lincoln's men?"

"Yes," says Mark Naper. "Bress Gawd, honey, I lube you, I can't tell how much I lubs you, glory, glory, glory!" And she made a rush for Mark, caught him in her big fat arms, and pulled him up close to her huge, greasy and nearly naked bosom and began to kiss him. Then she would hold him off at arm's length and yell, "Bress de Lawd, honey, ain't I happy. I lubs you, honey, I do!" and then she would pull him up and kiss him again.

Mark all this time was struggling to get away, and the boys were roaring with laughter and telling her, "Go on, old girl, that's just what he likes." Says she, "Ob corse I'se going on, Bress de Lawd," and then came another smack that sounded like a horse pulling a foot out of the mud.

No one ever saw a madder man than Mark was. He finally escaped from her and threatened to shoot some of us if we didn't "dry up," but it was no use. Someone would sing out, "Bress de Lawd!" and the whole company would roar. I do believe it was the funniest thing I ever saw. Mark was one of our best men and he was always just as clean as circumstances would allow. He hated dirt and filth, and for this particularly big, fat greasy wench to single him out was altogether too much for his temper.

It must have been about the last of May, 1865, when we finished our march and went into camp opposite the city of Washington. Our company and regiment, and in fact the whole army, at this time were made up of the best material. Our battles and marches, including this last one, had thinned us out. Many had been killed, many had died of sickness, many brave ones had died or been killed in prisons. Our skulkers had been gotten rid of, some to the ambulance corps, some with the teams. I think our company now had left, of the 105 men that left Chicago with us, only about thirty-five. And some of these had come to us from Chattanooga, not having started out with us. What was left of us were as tough as gristle. We were ragged and nearly barefooted. We had all kinds of head gear, regulation hats and caps, straw hats and wool hats.

For the last day or two of our march it had rained, and our camp was in a disagreeable place. We were camped about two miles from Alexandria, and we very soon had trouble. A spirit of rivalry, with a touch of dislike, existed between the West and the Army of the Potomac which served only in the East. They always went into winter quarters at the coming-on of winter. We campaigned right along, summer and winter, rain or shine. They did more fighting than we did, but compared with our work theirs was like taking all day to work in half a bushel.*

* Editor's note: What Strong means here apparently is that while the Army of the Potomac fought more great battles, Sherman's troops from the West were more constantly engaged in combat around the calendar. Basically this is correct. Certainly it is true of Strong, in view of his activities as skirmisher and forager.

In the spring, the Army of the Potomac advanced and had more severe battles than us, but winter found them about where they had begun in the spring. We, on the contrary, held any territory we gained and pushed on for more. They called us "water fowl" and "Sherman's Mules," all alluding to our long, wet marches. We called them "Feather Bed Soldiers," alluding to their being comfortably in camp so much. We also called them "White Collars" and "Soft Breads." The first of these was because they were regular dudes, wearing white collars and gloves and always well-clothed, clean and bright. We were dirty and ragged and barefooted and lousy and black with tan and exposure to all kinds of weather, but we were tough and not used to so much style.

Well, when we camped near Alexandria, we found every road and every bridge guarded by these white collar, soft bread soldiers in their white gloves. We were used to going where we pleased, when not on duty, and no questions asked as long as we were present at rollcall and ready for duty then. So we refused to acknowledge the authority of these white collar guards.

The day after we reached camp at Alexandria, a number of us started into Alexandria to see the town and the river. We had not gone far when we met a squad of six men who halted us and demanded our passes. We had none, so these guards attempted to arrest us. We told them we were going to the river, and if they meddled with us, we would buck and gag them. They did meddle with us, and we overpowered them, tied them with their handkerchiefs and gunslings, stacked their arms over their bent-down heads, and went on our way.

Next we came to a small stream with a bridge over it. Here the guards were too many for us. So we went back to camp, on the way releasing the guards that we had bucked and gagged. We warned them never to meddle with Sherman's Bummers again.

At camp, we gathered a big squad. We all took our sidearms, which with us infantry consisted mainly of bayonets, and marched to the heavily-guarded bridge. The guards halted us. We threw them into the creek. Most of the others went on to town, but I went back to camp. Guards along the road halted the others so often that they reached town hopping mad, and finally up and took the town. More guards came up and they came near having a real battle, but more bummers came and the guards were too few. Sherman's boys captured Alexandria from the Feather Bed Army of the Potomac, though you will find that fact in no history books at all.

A few days after we reached Alexandria, we learned there was to be a grand review of both the Army of the Potomac and of Sherman's Army. We received orders to apply for new uniforms to wear at the review. Almost to a man, we objected to this as we did not care to be out the expense of a new suit of clothes when we were at the end of the war and so near to going home. But the officers insisted, so we ordered enough new clothes to make us decent, but few of us drew hats or shoes. At the last moment, we refused to wear our new clothes on parade. Instead, we packed them away in our blanket rolls.

The Army of the Potomac had their review or parade through Washington on the first day, and we of the West on the next. It was a sight of splendor to see the Potomac boys. Their uniforms were brand new. Their shoes and belts were polished 'til they shone, their buckles and eagles (insignia) were bright as stars. They all wore white gloves and white collars. They marched with the short step, in perfect time, every foot moving in unison with comrades' feet. They were a splendid set of men, and were cheered by us and by the spectators.

Each regiment marched up to the grand stand in perfect time to music, then halted in front of the grand stand, which contained President Johnson and his Cabinet, General Grant, General Sherman and many others. It is, or was then, part of military drill that when the order to halt came on review or parade, every gun must come to "Right shoulder arms" in perfect time, none too slow, none too soon. This was done no matter what way we troops were carrying our guns, in one position or another as ordered, when the order to halt came. Each regiment on review came to "shoulder" perfectly. It was a sight to watch.

The second day, we of the West were trotted out to show off. Our uniforms were not new, and we wore all kinds of hats—but our guns were clean and bright. Our step was the long or route step of our marches, about six inches longer than the short step, and we moved in a sort of springy manner instead of with the stiff motion of the Eastern boys.

Instead of neat, well-packed knapsacks, we wore our blanket rolls over our shoulders as usual, with the ends tied together to make a big loop of blanket, the knotted end hanging down under our left arm. We were tanned and sunburnt. There was not a white collar or a pair of gloves among a thousand men. There was as great a contrast as possible between us and the "Feather Bed Soldiers," which was the way we wanted it, but we were every bit as well drilled.

We paraded with our heads held high up. Every man's eye was supposed to be fixed on his file leader's head, but I imagine we all saw all the pretty girls that were there lining the road. As our regiment came to a halt in front of the grand stand, it came without a word of command to a "shoulder." Then everybody cheered except us boys in the line. We stood there, apparently as indifferent as an old maid to the voice of flattery. All the same, we took it in.

At the next halt after our halt in front of the grand stand, reporters and citizens rushed up and asked, "What regiment is that?" They got all kinds of answers, such as "Hooker's Company, Sherman's Bummers, Sherman's Webfeet," and so on.

After the review, we did not recross the Potomac to our former camp, but went into camp near Fort Lincoln close to a small stream which emptied into the Potomac. As low tide this creek was shallow except in places. At high tide it became deep enough to swim a horse, and in the holes it was eight to ten feet deep. It was a grand swimming hole, but not all of our Western boys from beyond the tidewater recognized its dangers.

I was at the creek swimming, one evening just before rollcall, when the warning gun for rollcall fired. Everybody had to be in camp for rollcall. I think there must have been a thousand men there on the bank, all hurrying and dressing, when from the creek came a call for help. We looked. There were two men in one of those deep holes, hanging on to each other and calling for help. We all supposed they were fooling, of course—but they were not. Those two men actually drowned before thousands of men who would have helped them if they had not thought them to be playing.

While at Washington, we visited all the places of interest: The White House, Patent Office, and Treasury Building, among others. At the Treasury I saw a room bigger than your room, Mother, filled *full* with layers of uncut greenbacks, and another room, a vault, full of sacks of gold.

The Congress not being in session one morning, I sat in the Senate Chamber in the chair of the presiding officer and we boys held a mock session of Congress. In addressing one another, instead of saying the Member from Illinois, we would say the Comrade of the 105th Illinois, and so on.

While in Washington we drew the best of rations, soft bread instead of hard crackers, fresh meat and vegetables. With next to no duty to do, we all got fat. I weighed 185 pounds.

We kept up an almost continual quarrel with the Feather Bed fellows. If a lot of them met a smaller number of us, they thumped us. If we met them in the same circumstances, we did the same to them. Sometime on meeting a lot of us, they would begin to quack like ducks, referring to our nickname of Sherman's Webfoots. We would enquire after the health of their shiny buckles, white collars, etc. Many a boy got his head punched for being smart.

After the final grand review in Washington, Bob Strong and his comrades of the 105th Illinois entrained for home like triumphant heroes. At every stop, there were brass bands, bunting, and free lunches—until they got back to Chicago Then the bottom dropped out of their victory parade. Their last big battle took place in a beer garden.

homeward bound, but still fighting

WHEN WE received orders to march to the depot to take the train home, we were a happy set. At the depot we found some other troops going home, among them the 70th Illinois and a New Jersey regiment. The New Jersey regiment had already taken possession of enough cars to carry them comfortably. We were told to stand around and wait for more cars. The New Jersey boys began to taunt us from their cars. So we up and run them out of their cars. They got their guns and formed in line of battle with their colonel at their head. We left our guns stacked, but armed ourselves with stones. Their colonel and our Major Brown, who now commanded the regiment, came near having a row, but finally everything quieted down and other cars came.

We left Washington for Chicago singing, cheering and yelling, with everybody as happy and noisy as children. We passed through Baltimore and Pittsburgh and other large towns. At every city, we were made welcome and great measures were taken to feed us. Morning, noon or night, wherever the train stopped, we were greeted by bands of music and by processions of patriotic men, women, boys and girls, and escorted to some large hall where everything good to eat had been provided for us. These halls were decorated with flowers and with mottoes and words of welcome, such as "Welcome Our Brave Defenders." Of course under such treatment every man and boy was on his best behavior.

Everywhere along the way, we were met by banners and music. From farm houses, little flags were waved at us. I should have said that our engine and train also were nearly covered with banners. Old men and women, boys and girls, in villages and in the countryside waved at us.

As we neared Chicago, our colonel telegraphed the Mayor of the city to have quarters assigned to us. On reaching the city, we found neither quarters nor rations. Finally we camped without any supper. We had no money and could not buy anything to eat.

The next morning, we were ordered to quarters on the north side of the city—still without any breakfast or anything to eat. We took up our march across Chicago to camp. After being treated so well in strange cities, it made us all mad to be used this way in our home city. The ill feeling soon showed itself.

We marched along on the sidewalk. The police ordered us to take to the street and leave the walk for gentlemen. Someone pitched the policemen into the street head first, and we continued on the walk. A few of us fixed bayonets and constituted ourselves a rear guard. We fell behind so that we could not be seen from cross streets crossing the one we were on. After the regiment had passed and teams and pedestrians began to cross, we would charge at them with bayonets leveled. We took care not to hurt anyone, but many a slow man and several policemen were tumbled into the dirt. It was fun to see them run from those bayonets.

We reached our camp at nine o'clock Friday morning and found some rations had been sent to us. On opening the boxes of crackers, we found them alive with worms. The meat was so maggotty that we could not eat it. Then we were *mad!* Our officers bought us some dinner and the quartermaster was sent for. He attempted to apologize for the condition of the rations. He was told that if he did not very soon have full, clean rations on the grounds, we would *hang* him. The rations came, but we stayed mad.

That week I made application for a pass for two days to go home, but was told that no passes could be given. I then hunted up Jim George, who was in the hospital. I borrowed five dollars of him. I went back to see him again Saturday morning, and when I returned to quarters that night, I found the regiment had gone home to remain until Monday. I was too late to go.

(I am ashamed to record the following, but it comes next in the story, so I put it in.)

Adjoining our camp was a Dutch beer garden. On Sunday morning it began to fill up with men and women coming to spend the day drinking and dancing.

The other regiments in camp besides the 105th Illinois did not go home Saturday night, but went almost in a body into these beer gardens. Early on Sunday, a soldier in one of those regiments bought a whopping big glass of beer and drunk the health of "Old Billy Sherman." When this soldier toasted Old Billy, a big Dutchman said, "Damn Sherman." The soldier knocked him down with his beer glass. Others came to the Dutchman's rescue, and for a time I thought they would clean us out.

Just then, some soldier called out, "Attention, Sherman's Bummers to the rescue!" and then, Oh my countrymen, began a fierce fight. In ten minutes, the saloon keeper had not a bottle or keg or box of cigars unsmashed, and he himself lay senseless on the ground. Police came rushing in with their clubs, and they got a dubbing. The battle kept roaring for two hours. We did not go for our guns, but used our fists and chairs and the clubs which we had taken away from the policemen.

The Mayor—the same who had not provided a scrap of bread for our reception—ordered out all the police and himself came to quell the riot. He swore he would arrest every one of us. As it happened, General Joe Hooker, who had formerly had command of us, appeared about then. He told the Mayor: "These boys are mad at the way you have used them, but will quiet down if you let them alone. But if you bring any more policemen or new troops here, they will think it fun to whip the whole crowd. They have faced cannon and musketry for three years, and do not know what fear is. Let them alone or they will burn down your city."

So the Mayor let us alone. There was lots of talk among the boys of raiding the Copperhead city, but better counsel prevailed.

That night, as I had no one to go to for a pass, I took the matter into my own hands, went to the depot, got a ticket for Lemont, and started home. From Lemont I started to foot it home. In going from town, a man in a wagon passed me with a load of empty milk cans. I asked him for a ride. It was a bright night and he could see my uniform. He refused to let me ride and swore at me for a damned thieving bluecoat.

At that, I made a rush at him. He whipped up his horses and drove away from me. I went across the clover pasture near home, forded the creek, and came to the old spring. I climbed up on the fence and sat there a minute, a happy boy. I was thinking over whether to wake up the folks or sleep outside when I saw someone coming towards the spring. He knelt down to get a drink. When I spoke to him he looked up and said, "Is it Bob?" Says I, "Yes, it is Bob." It was Al, just getting home from sparking.

Well, Brother Al and I had a little hugging match right there by the spring and then went to the house. He says, "Pa, Ma, guess who's come home with me?" Father says, "Who is it?" and I says, "It's me!"

I think, Mother, that you never left your bed so quickly in your life as you did then. And then we all had another hugging match, all except Jennie. She was in bed and you would not let her be called.

Next morning I went to Naperville and returned to Chicago. There I was mustered out of the army on June 13, 1865. Getting back to Naperville on June 14th, I started to walk home. Mr. Walker overtook me and asked me to ride. He asked who I was, and when I told him he wanted to drive me straight around to our house. But I would not let him go out of his way. I remember how funny he looked at me the whole time, as if he thought I had a Rebel in my pocket.

I remember two things in particular after I got home for good. It was hard for me to sit in a chair or sleep in a bed. In the army, only captains and up had chairs. I hadn't sat in a chair in three years or about that. As for beds, they were too soft to sleep in. For a long time, I preferred to sleep and to sit on the floor.